In Tune with God's Word
Spiritual Themes for the Young Musician

By Ruth Meints

Copyright 2021 Ruth Meints
Published by Ruth Meints
In cooperation with A Powerful Story

Cover design by Tommy Owen and Gracie Flanigan
Interior design by Carol Davis
Author photo by May Yap Photography

Printed in the United States of America

All rights reserved. No part of this publication may be reproduced, stored in a retrieval system, or transmitted in any form or by any means—for example, electronic, photocopy, recording—without the prior written permission of the publisher.

The only exception is brief quotations in printed reviews.

Unless otherwise noted, all Scriptures are taken from THE HOLY BIBLE, NEW INTERNATIONAL VERSION®, NIV® Copyright © 1973, 1978, 1984, 2011 by Biblica, Inc.® Used by permission. All rights reserved worldwide.

Scriptures marked KJV are taken from the King James Version. Public domain.

ISBN 978-1-7369941-2-2

Dedication

*To my mom and dad
who raised me in an environment full of music
and love for the Lord Jesus Christ!*

ACKNOWLEDGEMENTS

I would like to thank all the devoted musical families who helped me with this project, including a special thanks to Amanda and Jared Abuhl for their input and support. Thank you to my dear friend Lydia Conway for her prayers, encouragement, and wise suggestions throughout the process.

Thank you to the members of my family for all their support in countless and extraordinary ways: My husband Ken, my parents Al and Judy Wilson, my sons Dryden, Aldric, and Skyler and their spouses, and my sister Paula.

Thank you to Jonathan Balzora, Lulrick Balzora, and Marie Claire Beauvil who passionately serve the Lord. They gave me huge encouragement to provide a way for young people to encounter God through their musical studies.

Thank you to Christ Community Church in Omaha and lead pastor, Mark Ashton, for providing a Christ-centered place to worship and fellowship. I am so grateful to Keri Wyatt Kent for her expert guidance through the editing and production of this devotional.

CONTENTS

Introduction 9
Quarter One 13
Week 1: Hope and a Future 15
Week 2: The Good Shepherd 19
Week 3: Build a Strong Foundation 23
Week 4: Two Types of Champions 27
Week 5: Natural and Spiritual. 31
Week 6: Freedom in Christ 35
Week 7: Keep Up the Good Work 39
Week 8: Praise Him With Music 43
Quarter One Review. 47
Quarter Two 49
Week 9: Attitude is Everything 51
Week 10: Don't Worry. 55
Week 11: Running Your Best Race 59
Week 12: Be Creative 63
Week 13: With All Your Heart 67
Week 14: A Willing Spirit 71
Week 15: The Messiah 75
Week 16: Rejoice! 79
Quarter Two Review. 83
Quarter Three 85

CONTENTS

Week 17: Have Courage! 87
Week 18: The New Is Here 91
Week 19: Show Me Your Ways 95
Week 20: A Roaring Lion 99
Week 21: The Armor of God 103
Week 22: Crossing the Red Sea 107
Week 23: Practice Performing 111
Week 24: Show Your Appreciation 115
Week 24: Show Your Appreciation 115
Quarter Three Review 119
Quarter Four 121
Week 25: Superhero Skills 123
Week 26: All Things Work Together 127
Week 27: Citizen of Heaven 131
Week 28: Relying on God 135
Week 29: Following Directions 139
Week 30: Fishers of Men 143
Week 31: The Advocate 147
Week 32: A Good Work 151
Quarter Four Review 155
About the Author 157
About String Sprouts 159

INTRODUCTION

A cord of three strands is not quickly broken. (Ecclesiastes 4:12)

A note to parents:

Your choice to embark upon a musical journey with your family is a beautiful thing! The study of music has been shown to benefit academic outcomes, bolster social skills, and build strong character needed for success in life.

By choosing to use this devotional alongside your child's musical training, you are bringing spiritual formation into the process. No matter what programs and activities we engage in throughout our life, little else compares to eternal outcomes. To that end, this devotional weaves spiritual truths into each week of music-making. It will equip each parent with a variety of teaching tools and activities to bring awareness to the things of God in your everyday life. Both you and your child will develop a sense of gratefulness and reliance on Jesus Christ in everything you do. As Ecclesiastes 4:12 says, "A cord of three strands is not easily broken." This threefold cord—made up of you, your child, and God—will produce a life-changing experience that helps your child develop noble character and spiritual strength.

After your child attends their individual lesson or music class each week, you can use the devotional to enrich their practice sessions throughout the week. Each spiritual theme connects to the study of a musical instrument in some way. When we play music, our entire brain is activated, so when we learn a spiritual truth and attach it to musical material, we absorb it in a much deeper way.

Each week, you and your child will learn both a Bible verse and a vocabulary word. You'll then dive a bit deeper by reading a longer Bible passage together, and then considering ways to apply what you've read, and how to connect these spiritual truths to your child's musical education.

This 32-week devotional is divided into four quarters of eight weeks each. At the end of each quarter, you'll review and celebrate your progress and set goals for the next quarter. It can be used alongside the String Sprouts curriculum, but it doesn't have to be. Use it in whatever way serves your family and your young musician.

I encourage you to use as many of these tools and ideas as you possibly can throughout each week. I hope that your family has a warm, rich musical journey. But even beyond the musical experience, I pray that your relationship with the Lord Jesus Christ grows deeper and deeper through the intersection with music study and this devotional. Blessings to you and your family!

Ruth Meints

HOW TO USE THIS FAMILY DEVOTIONAL

The material provided in each week's devotional can be integrated into the daily practice and used in a variety of ways throughout the week. Here are some suggestions for how to incorporate these spiritual activities in a meaningful way.

- *Memory verse:* Start each practice session by reviewing the memory verse. If the verse can be broken into smaller pieces, work on memorizing smaller segments and then connecting them in the same way you would memorize a piece of music. As you work on your musical material, you will tie together the repertoire, devotional material, and scripture to create yet another "threefold cord."

- *Word of the Week:* The more vocabulary a child learns in the early years, the more likely they are to be successful once they reach school age. These vocabulary words will give your child a deeper understanding of what they are learning as they read the Bible. Try to use the Word of the Week in conversation as much as possible. Have your young musician draw a picture that represents the word to them. Also, create a partner card with the Word of the Week written on it. Eventually, you can play a game of concentration with these cards, matching the printed word to the picture they've drawn.

- *In Tune with God's Word:* Spend several days reading the Bible passage together before you read the Spiritual Themes section. After your child becomes familiar with it, try acting out the story or creating a scene that shows the meaning of the passage in action. See if your young musician(s) can tell the story in their own words. If the story has characters, find action figures or make puppets, dolls, or stick figures to represent these people. Use them as you tell the story in your own words or reread the passage. Reread throughout the week to keep the spiritual content at the forefront as your child practices their instrument daily.

- *Spiritual Themes:* As a parent or caregiver, you should read the devotional segment yourself to prepare for the week. Spend time in prayer, asking God to help you present the ideas in the clearest and most age-appropriate way for your young musician to understand

and grow spiritually. Depending upon the age of your child, you might read the Spiritual Theme together, or you may just explain it in a way you know they'll understand. Afterwards, spend time talking about its meaning and application to daily life, as well as answering any questions that come up. For a younger child, you might need to highlight a few key sentences and break up the material into smaller chunks, similar to the memory verse.

- *Playing from the Heart:* Help your child put each idea into action during their practice time. Read the questions to your child, and invite them to discuss their thoughts with you. These ideas bring the spiritual themes into the action of daily life. Applying God's word is the most important step in growing spiritually. When Jesus spoke about the seed falling on different types of soil, He said, "Others, like seed sown on good soil, hear the word, accept it, and produce a crop—some thirty, some sixty, some a hundred times what was sown" (Mark 4:20). Spiritual applications, combined with the musical experiences of practice and performance, help plant seeds in your child's heart.

- *Praying from the Heart:* At the end of each practice time, use the prayer to spend time together with God. This prayer is just a starting point! Add your own prayers of thanks, praise, and requests!

- *My Music Journal:* Each week includes some space for your child to make notes on progress, record goals or accomplishments, or write down a highlight from what they learned that week.

WEEK 1
HOPE AND A FUTURE

 **MEMORY VERSE**

For I know the plans I have for you; plans to prosper you and not to harm you, plans to give you hope and a future. (Jeremiah 29:11)

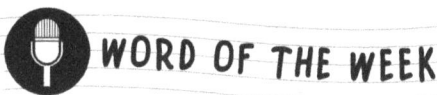 **WORD OF THE WEEK**

PROSPER: to cause to succeed or thrive

 **IN TUNE WITH GOD'S WORD**

Read Psalm 139:1-16.

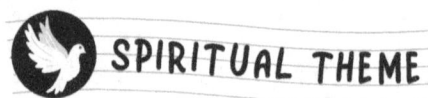

SPIRITUAL THEME

Have you or someone in your family ever made something by knitting or sewing? When a knitter begins a project, whether they are knitting a sweater, cap or scarf, they usually start with a pattern. This pattern gives specific directions to create a beautiful end result. Whatever it will be when it is finished, the plan exists. The pattern will help create the item the creator of the pattern envisioned.

In the same way, God has a plan for your life. You are special! In the Psalms we read: "For you created my inmost being; you knit me together in my mother's womb" (Psalm 139:13). God knew all about you before you were born and he has a fantastic life planned for you. In fact, God said, "For I know the plans I have for you; plans to prosper you and not to harm you, plans to give you hope and a future" (Jeremiah 29:11).

It's pretty exciting to know that the God of the universe created a pattern to create you and His plans for you include success, safety, and an awesome future.

PLAYING FROM THE HEART

1. Each time you practice a piece of music, you are following a pattern written by the composer to bring their musical ideas to life. You have been made in the image of God and are exactly the way God wanted you to be! God's pattern for you was designed and brought to life perfectly. Each time you play a piece, take a moment to thank God for weaving a beautiful pattern that created YOU!

2. God cares about the small details of His plans. Practice getting into playing position for your instrument. Follow each of the steps carefully, paying attention to every detail. What is the plan your

teacher gave you for at-home practice? Create a practice plan for each day and then make it a reality by finishing each task. Use the music journal area below to indicate something you improved on this week because of your practice.

3. God plans to keep you safe and not to harm you. What are some ways you can keep your instrument safe? When you finish practicing, clean your instrument and practice putting it away correctly. Protect your instrument from harm by keeping it in a safe place, just like God protects you!

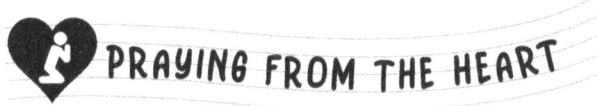 PRAYING FROM THE HEART

Thank you, Jesus, for creating a pattern that made me exactly the way you planned. Thank you for giving me hope because you have a plan for my future!

WEEK 2
THE GOOD SHEPHERD

 **MEMORY VERSE**

"I am the good shepherd; I know my sheep and my sheep know me." (John 10:14)

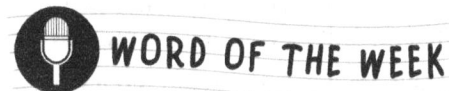 **WORD OF THE WEEK**

SHEPHERD: a person who takes care of sheep

 **IN TUNE WITH GOD'S WORD**

Read John 10:11-18.

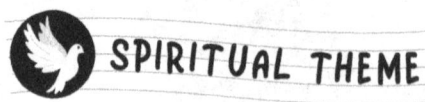
SPIRITUAL THEME

Imagine you are playing outside, and suddenly someone calls your name. If it is your mom, dad or best friend, you probably know who it is before you look up and see them. You recognize their voice because you know them well.

Jesus said that our friendship with him should be like that! When we get to know him, we recognize His voice. Jesus said, "I am the good shepherd; I know my sheep and my sheep know me…" (John 10:14). Jesus cares about you and patiently draws you to Himself. "He is patient with you, not wanting anyone to perish, but everyone to come to repentance" (2 Peter 3:9).

We learn to recognize a voice by listening carefully to it, as well as hearing it frequently—as we do with our family and close friends. In a similar way, when we learn to play a new piece, we have to listen to the rhythms and sounds repetitively to learn how the piece goes. After we know how the piece goes, we still need to develop our deeper listening skills to hear the details of the piece.

God loves to spend time with you every day. The more time you spend with God, the more quickly you will learn to know His voice. By reading the Bible every day, you have direct access to what God has said. As you become more familiar with what God has said, you will begin to know His voice when He reminds you of things you've read in the Bible.

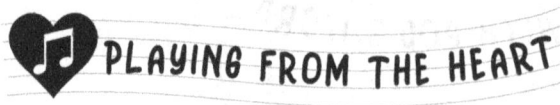
PLAYING FROM THE HEART

1. As a young musician, listening is an extremely important part of developing your ears. The great masters of your instrument can teach you a lot through their performances. Can you name three

well-known performers on your instrument? The more you listen, the more you will know the sound of rich tone, the balance of melody and harmony, and the shape of a beautiful phrase. God is our shepherd, and our role as sheep is simply to listen for His loving voice. Thank Him for being a good shepherd who cares about YOU!

2. Spend time listening to music every day. Developing a daily practice of listening will help you recognize whether or not what you are playing on your instrument sounds the same as what you are hearing on the recording. Spending time with God every day through Bible reading is the same. You will develop the same ability to know whether your actions are lining up with God's direction in His word. Did you listen to the piece you are learning today? Make a listening checklist and a Bible-reading checklist for the week.

3. God wants you to know His voice so He can teach you how to live a godly life. In your daily life, practice listening carefully to your teachers—whether that be your parents, classroom teachers, music teacher, or any regular caregiver in your life. Being a good listener is the first step to being a good learner.

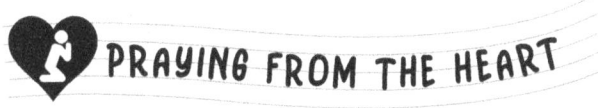
PRAYING FROM THE HEART

Dear Jesus, thank you for taking care of me, like a shepherd takes care of his sheep. Teach me through your words in the Bible. I want to know your voice.

WEEK 3
BUILD A STRONG FOUNDATION

 **MEMORY VERSE**

Therefore everyone who hears these words of mine and puts them into practice is like a wise man who built his house on the rock. (Matthew 7:24)

 **WORD OF THE WEEK**

PRACTICE: to train by repeated exercises

 **IN TUNE WITH GOD'S WORD**

Read Matthew 7:24-27.

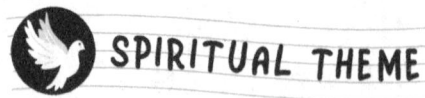 ## SPIRITUAL THEME

Have you ever built a sandcastle at the beach? No matter how beautiful that sandcastle is, when the tide comes in, it will be easily washed away.

A real house needs a solid foundation. If you try to build a house on shifting sand or unstable ground, it will not last when the storms arrive.

The idea of a house built on solid ground gives us a picture of what our life is like. If you want to be a follower of Jesus Christ, you have to hear His word and put it into practice. When you practice something, you do it over and over again, until you become an expert. By listening to God and practicing what He tells you to do, you build a solid foundation for your walk with the Lord.

Notice that in both situations, the builders found themselves in a storm. The builder whose house stood firm was the one who had built on the rock. Jesus explained that this stronger house was a picture of someone who practiced reading the Word of God and doing it. They were in the habit of relying on God's word to help them make it through the storms of life.

The house that was built on the sand wasn't able to stand up against the storm. This is a picture of someone who hears God's Word, but doesn't do what it says. They go through life doing whatever they want. When the hard times come, they are in big trouble because they don't have a relationship with God.

James, the brother of Jesus, gives us another great example. "Anyone who listens to the word but does not do what it says is like someone who looks at his face in a mirror and, after looking at himself, goes away and immediately forgets what he looks like. But whoever looks intently into the perfect law that gives freedom, and continues in it—not forgetting what they have heard, but doing it—they will be blessed in what they do" (James 1: 23-25). The mirror can tell you if you've got messy hair or dirt on your face. It's a great way to examine yourself. If reading God's word is like looking in a mirror, it will give you directions for how to live your life in a way that is pleasing to God. But there's only one way you will actually look your best when you are out in the world living your life! You have to follow the directions you've been given in God's word.

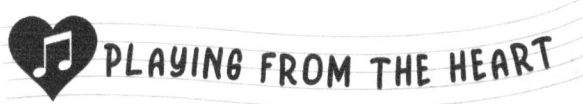

PLAYING FROM THE HEART

1. When we practice something, we become really good at it. How many times can you play your piece this week? Keep a tally of how many times you play it. As you get rock solid in your ability to play the piece, it won't matter what the circumstances are, you will be able to play it well! You won't be bothered by a surprise performance or any other musical storm that comes your way.

2. The Bible will always give you directions about how to live a life pleasing to God. In the same way, your music teacher will give you directions about what things you need to improve in order to play your instrument well. After each lesson or class, make a list of things you need to practice and make a plan with your parent or caregiver to put your instructions into practice. The more you practice, the stronger your foundation!

3. What was the most important thing you learned during your music class this week? What was the main point of the lesson for you? There may be a new piece to learn. That's an obvious thing to include in your practice plan, but there may be things that are less obvious that you need to focus on, too. Was there anything about how to hold or play your instrument that you need to remember? Depending on your instrument, do you need to improve or change the shape of your hands or mouth when you are playing? Is there anything you need to do that will improve your tone quality? Be careful to pay attention to all of the small details your teacher mentioned!

PRAYING FROM THE HEART

Thank you for giving us Your Word, so we can know how to live our lives following your example. I want to be a hearer and a doer of Your Word!

MY MUSIC JOURNAL

WEEK 4
TWO TYPES OF CHAMPIONS

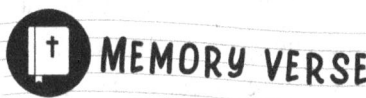
MEMORY VERSE

Since you are my rock and my fortress, for the sake of your name lead and guide me. (Psalm 31:3)

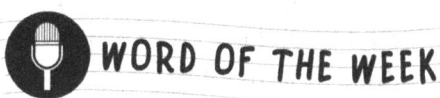
WORD OF THE WEEK

CHAMPION: a person who has defeated or surpassed all rivals

IN TUNE WITH GOD'S WORD

Read 1 Samuel 17:1-51.

# SPIRITUAL THEME

Goliath was a really BIG guy and a really BIG deal as the champion of the Philistine army. In order to be a champion, he had likely dedicated a lot of his time to achieving excellence in specific skills. In this case, as part of the military, Goliath was really good at fighting.

When a person gets really good at a certain skill, they can choose to act one of two ways: they can be prideful and arrogant, or they can be humble and helpful. Often, when someone chooses the first route, their amazing skills are overshadowed by their bullying and ugly attitude. Goliath relied on his own skills and pridefully bragged about how great he was, even defying God. When David approached him, Goliath said, "Am I a dog, that you come at me with sticks?" And the Philistine cursed David by his gods (1 Samuel 17:43). He definitely chose to be prideful and arrogant.

In total contrast, David chose a humble and helpful attitude. As a result, he became the true champion. He remembered his many successes as a shepherd out in the field. He knew God was preparing him for the future with each difficult challenge he faced. David knew through these experiences that he could trust the Lord to help him meet any challenge, no matter how difficult it might be. When the Israelites' King Saul outlined all the reasons that David should be concerned about fighting Goliath, David responded, "The Lord who rescued me from the paw of the lion and the paw of the bear will rescue me from the hand of this Philistine" (1 Sam. 17:37).

David knew he could help the Israelites, and he stood up for what was right, rather than being afraid of a bully. He boldly declared to everyone that he would defeat Goliath. Goliath's defeat would show both the Israelites and Philistines that the battle is the Lord's and not won by swords, spears, or any other man-made strategy.

Once it was clear that David would fight Goliath, Saul offered David some things he thought might help: his armor, helmet, and sword.

David immediately decided that he wouldn't rely on the equipment that was usually used in a confrontation of this sort. Instead, he would use his own tried-and-true equipment and skills and God's help to win the battle. He had spent years practicing with his slingshot when he was tending his father's flock. He came to the fight prepared with five stones he had chosen, even though he ended up needing only one of them. David's size, experience, and tools didn't matter as much as his reliance on the biggest rock of all, the God of the universe.

Even though the stone in David's slingshot seemed small in comparison to the size of the challenge, he won the battle because God was helping him. Someone who is considered a "rock" is described as strong, stable, and dependable. The memory verse talks about God being our Rock because He is a trustworthy, secure champion who can guide and lead us through any challenge we might be facing.

PLAYING FROM THE HEART

1. Since all of our abilities are God-given, we honor Him when we use our skills to make the world a better place. How can you bring joy to someone's life by sharing your new musical voice? As you develop your musical skills, find ways to use them for the glory of God. Maybe you could play at an assisted living center, perform at a hospital, or entertain shoppers at a farmer's market. Find a way to share your God-given talents!

2. Always be prepared! David brought five stones to a challenge, when he could have brought only one. He was thinking ahead about what he might need. If you play all of your review pieces, as well as all your current pieces, it prepares you for any "spur of the moment" performances when you could bless someone with your music. When you practice, don't settle for the bare minimum. Go the extra mile! How many review pieces can you play this week? Set a goal, and make it happen!

3. God can be trusted to help us with big challenges. You can and should ask God to guide and lead you through whatever difficult situation or circumstance you are experiencing. Thank God for being a solid Rock and the Ultimate Champion for you to hold onto with confidence!

PRAYING FROM THE HEART

Dear Jesus, Thank you for guiding and leading me! You are my Rock and the Ultimate Champion. Thankfully, with your help, I can meet any challenge with confidence. Praise the Lord!

MY MUSIC JOURNAL

WEEK 5
NATURAL AND SPIRITUAL

 **MEMORY VERSE**

For God so loved the world that he gave his one and only Son, that whoever believes in him shall not perish but have eternal life. (John 3:16)

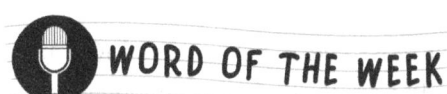 **WORD OF THE WEEK**

ETERNAL: lasting forever

 **IN TUNE WITH GOD'S WORD**

Read John 3:1-21.

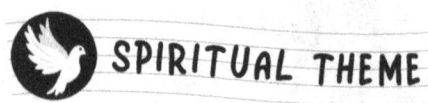 SPIRITUAL THEME

What day is your birthday? Your birthday was a very special day for your family--the day you became the newest member of your family on earth. When Jesus was on earth, He let us know that there could be another special day—our spiritual birthday! This is the day when your spirit is born into God's heavenly family to live forever with Him.

Nicodemus believed Jesus was a great teacher and that God was with Him. He wanted to learn from Jesus, so he asked a lot of important questions. As they talked, Jesus told Nicodemus that he would need to be born again. Nicodemus wondered what Jesus meant. How could a grownup be a baby again?

Jesus explained to him, "Very truly I tell you, no one can enter the kingdom of God unless they are born of water and the Spirit. Flesh gives birth to flesh, but the Spirit gives birth to spirit" (John 3:6-7). When Nicodemus realized Jesus was talking about a spiritual birth, he wanted to know how this second birth of the spirit could take place.

Then, Jesus Christ shared the best news ever! "For God so loved the world that he gave his one and only Son, that whoever believes in him shall not perish but have eternal life" (John 3:16).

Jesus Christ came to make a way for each of us to become part of His spiritual family. When you believe that Jesus Christ died on the cross for the sins of the whole world and rose again on the third day, you will experience your second birthday for your spirit! Jesus, the life-giving Spirit, gives your spirit eternal life, and you are born into the spiritual family of Jesus Christ. What a great day!

Have you believed in the Lord Jesus Christ? When you do, let Jesus know through prayer that you believe in Him. You can use the prayer in the Praying from the Heart section. After you do, make sure you let someone know about your spiritual birthday! They will want to celebrate with you!

PLAYING FROM THE HEART

1. Each time you play your piece, you are getting closer to the day when you will be able to perform it not only with all the right notes and rhythms, but also with feeling and emotion. We are each born into the world as a baby and have the chance to have a second birth of our spirit. When we learn a piece, the process is similar. Our piece is like a baby when we start it. If we keep working on the piece, we will get to a point where we can add the emotions and spirit to the piece. If we stop too soon, we won't experience the joy of fully knowing a piece of music. Every time you practice this week, thank God for making a way for our spirits to come alive through belief in Him!

2. To learn a new piece, we first need to be able to do the physical skills needed to play it. How do I play or sing the rhythms and notes in the piece correctly? After you have mastered the basic elements of the piece, you can start to think about expressing an idea, mood, or story through your playing. Learning a piece of music has the same progression as life, moving from the natural (notes and rhythms) to the spiritual (what feeling you are sharing with this piece of music). What stage are you in for each of your pieces? If you are in the "natural" phase, make a plan to improve the elements of notes and rhythms that you need to fix in order to move to the next level. If you are in the "spiritual" stage, make a plan to improve the phrasing, dynamics, and characters throughout each section. Ask your teacher or parent if you need help planning a practice session that fits your level of growth on each piece. Take time to write your plans in the music journal for each piece you are working on.

3. Have you believed in the life-giving Spirit, Jesus Christ? Make that decision today! Ask God to breathe spiritual life into you! Does your

spirit need to be awakened so you can join the spiritual family of Jesus?

PRAYING FROM THE HEART

Dear Jesus, I believe You died and rose again for my sins. I know my natural body will die at some point, but my spirit will have eternal life with You. Thank you for bringing me into your spiritual family!

MY MUSIC JOURNAL

WEEK 6
FREEDOM IN CHRIST

 **MEMORY VERSE**

Now the Lord is the Spirit, and where the Spirit of the Lord is, there is freedom. (2 Corinthians 3:17)

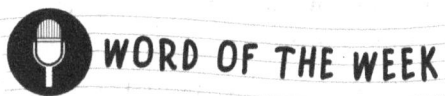 **WORD OF THE WEEK**

FREEDOM: the power to act, speak or think without restriction

 **IN TUNE WITH GOD'S WORD**

Read Exodus 1:7-14 and Exodus 12:31-36.

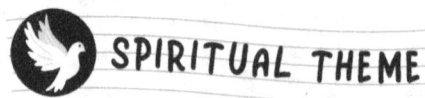 SPIRITUAL THEME

The Israelites were God's people. They spent their days working hard to build pyramids and other city buildings for the Egyptian rulers.

Slaves have to do things they don't want to do. They suffer because of being slaves. The Bible sometimes says we are "slaves to sin." What does that mean? Sometimes, even though we want to do what is right, we do the wrong thing. Sin makes us do things we don't want to do, as if we were slaves to it. As a result, we suffer.

Even though the Israelites were slaves to the Egyptians, God had a plan to bring them out of their slavery. In an extraordinary demonstration of God's power through the ten plagues, Pharaoh finally called for the leaders of the Israeli slaves, Moses and Aaron, and told them to leave Egypt with all of the people of Israel.

God had a plan for His people then, and He still does today. Romans 8:28 says, "And we know that in all things God **works for** the **good** of those who love him, who have been called according to his purpose." Every person is in slavery before they commit their lives to the Lord, because everyone is separated from God by a sinful nature. The primary goal in life for every person is to reconnect with God. We all need to leave our sinful nature behind and place our trust in Jesus Christ who can give us freedom and guidance through life.

 PLAYING FROM THE HEART

1. Making a plan is one of the best things you can do to achieve success. Make a plan for your next practice session that includes five things you want to practice. Ask yourself these two questions about each piece you're practicing:

- What do I need to improve? (Maybe it's to improve a technical skill or maybe it's to improve your musical interpretation.)

- How will I practice this? (What method will you use to practice? It could be repetition of a small segment or perhaps practicing with a metronome for better rhythm.)

2. Choose a tricky passage to practice ten times. As you play each repetition, remember how God protected the Israelites from the plagues, which God brought upon the Egyptians. When you reach the final repetition, make sure to have a special celebration because the Israelites were freed from slavery and eventually God brought them into a new land of their own.

3. Every time you practice a tricky passage until you can play it without mistakes, you've moved yourself from technical struggle to musical freedom. Let these successes remind you about the wonderful news that God wants to bring you out of slavery to total freedom, just like he had a plan to bring the Israelites out of bondage in Egypt.

PRAYING FROM THE HEART

Dear Jesus, I have put my trust in You, and I thank You for the freedom I have in Christ.

WEEK 7
KEEP UP THE GOOD WORK

 **MEMORY VERSE**

Let perseverance finish its work so that you may be mature and complete, not lacking anything. (James 1:4)

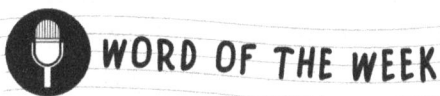 **WORD OF THE WEEK**

PERSEVERANCE: the effort required to do something and keep doing it until the end, even if it's hard

 **IN TUNE WITH GOD'S WORD**

Read Genesis Chapters 6-8.

 ## SPIRITUAL THEME

The people of the earth had become so wicked that God decided to bring a flood over the whole earth. But because Noah was a faithful follower of God, God rescued him. God gave Noah a plan about how to build the ark, a giant boat, big enough to hold his whole family and all the animals. God warned Noah about what was coming and provided a way for Noah to protect his family, as well as all the different types of animals.

The flood was a really hard thing to live through, but Noah and his family made it with God's guidance. Often when we experience difficult circumstances, we ask God to make it go away. God doesn't always answer our prayer by bringing us out of it, but rather He brings us through it! We can trust God in every circumstance. In James 1:2-4, it says we should "Consider it pure joy, whenever you face trials of many kinds, because the testing of your faith produces perseverance. Let perseverance finish its work so that you may be mature and complete, not lacking anything. "

As we experience hardships and make it through them with God's help, we strengthen our faith in how God works in our lives and always provides what we need and a way through the challenge.

 ## PLAYING FROM THE HEART

1. Learning to play an instrument well takes a long time. Noah was on the ark for a long time, too. The Bible says it rained for 40 days and 40 nights. But Noah persevered and exited the ark with the animals into a new world. Make a "Noah's ark" practice chart. Practice for 40 days without missing a day to understand how long Noah and his family were on the ark while it was raining. After it

WEEK 8
PRAISE HIM WITH MUSIC

MEMORY VERSE

It is good to praise the Lord and make music to your name, O Most High. (Psalm 92:1)

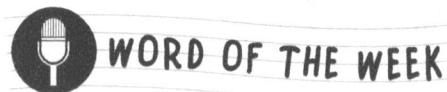
WORD OF THE WEEK

CELEBRATION: a joyful occasion for special festivities to mark some happy event

IN TUNE WITH GOD'S WORD

Read Psalm 92.

SPIRITUAL THEME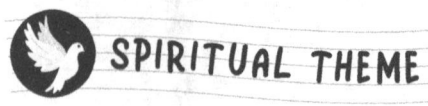

Music is almost always an essential part of any celebration. From singing "Happy Birthday" to caroling at Christmas, we add music to make our celebrations even more special. In the Bible, music played a big role in many important events.

When Solomon brought the ark into the temple, it says, "The trumpeters and musicians joined in unison to give praise and thanks to the Lord" (2 Chronicles 5:13). After David killed Goliath, Saul and the Israelite army returned home where "the women came out from all the towns of Israel to meet King Saul with singing and dancing, with joyful songs and with timbrels and lyres" (1 Samuel 18:6). When Jesus celebrated Passover with his disciples, they sang a hymn before going out to the Mount of Olives (Matthew 26:30).

Every eight weeks, this devotional will provide a chance to honor all the work that you have put into learning your instrument. It's also a chance to praise the Lord! We can be sure that our music makes God happy. "From palaces adorned with ivory the music of the strings makes you glad" (Psalm 45:8). Celebrate with joy your musical accomplishments, and bring a smile to God's face!

PLAYING FROM THE HEART

1. Celebrate the completion of the first quarter. Think of eight things you can do now that you couldn't do eight weeks ago. That's some great progress and a huge amount of learning! Which skills are your very best? Was there a challenge that gave you a struggle but now you can do it? Give thanks to God for the opportunity to learn an instrument!

2. Review each piece you have learned starting from week one

and practice saying the memory verse for that week. Plan a special home concert or performance in the community where you say your memory verses and play your pieces. Practice walking onto the stage area, taking a bow, and getting ready to play your instrument. Play each piece with a beautiful sound. When you say your memory verses, send your voice to the back of the performance space by speaking loudly and clearly.

3. Ask your parent or caregiver to tell you a story about how God has been faithful in their lives. Find out which of your pieces is their favorite, and play it in celebration of God's faithfulness.

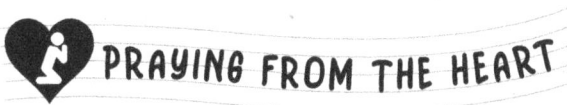
PRAYING FROM THE HEART

Dear Lord, I am thankful for the chance to learn to play an instrument. Thank you for Your help every day and faithfulness to me and my family. We praise Your name with our instruments and voices!

Quarter One Review

List eight new skills you learned in the last eight weeks:

1.
2.
3.
4.
5.
6.
7.
8.

WEEK 9
ATTITUDE IS EVERYTHING

 **MEMORY VERSE**

Be kind and compassionate to one another, forgiving each other, just as in Christ God forgave you. (Ephesians 4:32)

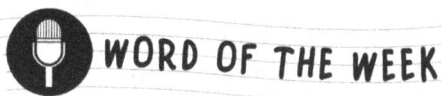 **WORD OF THE WEEK**

ATTITUDE: a state of mind

 **IN TUNE WITH GOD'S WORD**

Read Ephesians 4:29-32.

 SPIRITUAL THEME

Have you ever had a day when you were grumpy or not in a good mood? There are times we feel sad or mad—that's just part of life. But when you're feeling bad, you can talk to God. Tell Him how you're feeling. Ask for His help, so that you don't make other people around you feel bad, too!

One of the most important things we can learn in life is that we have control over our attitude. In every situation, we get to choose whether we will be kind or mean, friendly or unfriendly, helpful or unhelpful, grumpy or pleasant. Decide today you will not be a "Little Grumpus!"

God tells us clearly what our attitude goals should be every day. The apostle Paul writes to the Ephesians, "Get rid of all bitterness, rage and anger, brawling and slander, along with every form of malice." These are all emotions that would fall into the category of "bad attitudes." How can we get rid of that bad attitude? Paul has some great ideas: Be kind to others. Be compassionate towards others. Be forgiving to anyone who may have shown a "bad attitude" towards you in their actions. You may not feel like being kind, but when you do, you'll be surprised how it makes you feel better!

We want to become more and more like Christ each day. If we keep in mind how much we have been forgiven by God, it will make us much more merciful and compassionate towards other people. God's attitude towards each one of us is full of compassion, flooded with kindness, and overwhelmingly merciful in spite of our sinful nature, so this fact should make us extend the same love to other people.

 PLAYING FROM THE HEART

1. If you are grumpy during a practice session, stop for a moment. Why are you sad or mad? Decide that you are going to change your thinking. Think about three things for which you would like to thank God. When you have finished thanking God out loud for these three things, determine whether you are still grumpy. Keep on thanking God for all He has given you until your attitude has changed. You can thank Him for the smallest to the biggest of blessings. Then, you can go back to the practice session once you have kicked your "Little Grumpus" out of the room!

2. After each practice session, rate your attitude and effort. Did you get a sad face for being difficult and unhappy during practice? Did you get a "meh" face for showing very little effort and not really giving your all? Or did you get a smiley face for excellent effort and attitude? See how many smiley faces you can get this week! Use your music journal to record your attitude ratings this week.

3. When you play your pieces, think about your stage presence. Try playing in front of a mirror. Does your face look inviting when you play? Are you preparing to play your instrument in a way that shows good energy and alertness? Are your eyes focused on the right place, so the audience will not be distracted and can listen to your beautiful music? How we look on the stage adds so much to the performance and the audience's enjoyment!

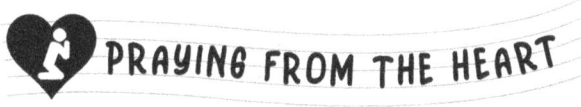 PRAYING FROM THE HEART

Jesus, Thank You for saving me! Thank You for creating me in your image! Thank You for creating all the plants and animals! Thank You for the gift of music! Thank You for watching over me each day! Thank You for _____! (How many different things can you thank the Lord for today?)

 MY MUSIC JOURNAL

WEEK 10
DON'T WORRY!

MEMORY VERSE

Cast all your anxiety on Him because He cares for you. (1 Peter 5:7)

WORDS OF THE WEEK

ANXIOUS: to be worried, nervous, or uneasy, about an event or something with an uncertain outcome

PRAYER: a solemn request for help or expression of thanks addressed to God

IN TUNE WITH GOD'S WORD

Read Matthew 14:22-33.

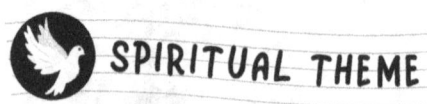
SPIRITUAL THEME

Peter had faith to do something incredible—walk on water. He was willing to step out of the boat onto the surface of the water and meet Jesus there. Even though he successfully walked on the water for a short time, he became afraid and anxious about making it to Jesus after he began to focus on the wind whipping around him. He started to sink into the water the moment he took his eyes off Jesus, but he did have the presence of mind to pray. He called to Jesus, "Lord, save me!" Immediately, Jesus was there to pull him out of the water.

Life is full of uncertainty. Whenever we are afraid or anxious, the Lord offers a way to keep us from going underwater and getting overwhelmed by the circumstances we are facing. In 1 Peter 5:7, Peter teaches us a good thing to do: Cast all your anxiety on Him because He cares for you. The best way to give your anxiety to Jesus is through prayer. "Do not be anxious about anything, but in every situation, by prayer and petition, with thanksgiving, present your requests to God" (Philippians 4:6).

Relying on God in every situation helps calm the fear of what lies ahead. Jesus cares about us in a big way and will be there to help, support, and save us, if we keep our eyes fixed on Him.

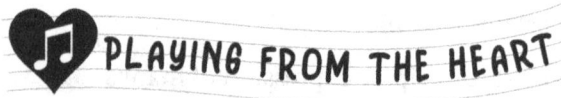
PLAYING FROM THE HEART

1. It's easier to navigate any circumstance in our lives when we focus steadily on Jesus Christ. This concept of focus can be applied to playing our instrument. Keep your eyes focused on what you are doing, when you play your instrument. For example, look at your instrument as you play it. Don't let your eyes wander. Think about what you are doing. If your focus is steady, you will be far more likely to play accurately with fewer mistakes. Practice keeping your eyes

focused on your instrument while playing. Your parent or caregiver can make a silly noise or use a bell or whistle to bring your focus back if it starts to fade. Can you play through your entire piece without getting distracted?

2. Whenever you feel overwhelmed by something in your practice session, take a break to ask God for help and also give thanks for the opportunity to learn an instrument, just like it says to do in Philippians 4:6. God is always there to hear your prayer and remove your anxiety, if you rely on Him.

3. Often when we struggle with something, it's because we are focusing our attention on the wrong thing. When you start a practice segment, set a goal and determine your focus. Whatever you choose to work on, don't let any other issues that arise distract you from your main focus. You will get more done if you don't try to fix everything all at once and keep your attention on a single goal until you finish it.

PRAYING FROM THE HEART

Dearest Jesus, when I am worried about something, I know I can pray for Your help in any situation. As I keep my focus on You, I will give thanks for Your presence with me.

WEEK 11
RUNNING YOUR BEST RACE

 **MEMORY VERSE**

Do you not know that in a race all the runners run, but only one gets the prize? Run in such a way as to get the prize. (1 Corinthians 9:24)

 **WORD OF THE WEEK**

CONSISTENT: free from variation or change

 **IN TUNE WITH GOD'S WORD**

Read Hebrews 11:1-12:3.

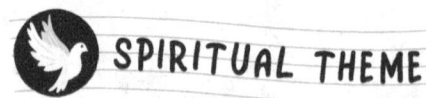
SPIRITUAL THEME

Have you ever had to run a long race? Did you take any steps to prepare for the race to increase your chances of winning or making it to the end? Preparing well to run a race requires a long-term plan and consistent practice. What would you need to do if you wanted to have a chance at winning a race? Without a doubt, you would have to develop enough stamina to make it the whole distance. You wouldn't be able to finish if you decided to start jogging a day before the race. If your goal was to win, you'd also have to study how others who came before you won the race. What's a typical winning time? How did these past champions prepare? Lastly, you'd have to be consistent about your practice over a long period of time to be as ready as possible when the day of the race arrives.

In the memory verse, Paul tells us there will be many runners who are "running for God." Being consistent in our spiritual walk will develop stronger faith and more reliance on God. Whenever we want to be inspired about how to run the "race of life" or if we become discouraged or tired, we should read through Hebrews 11 to find out about all the people who have gone before us and run their life's race well with consistency and focus.

One of the best ways to become an expert at something is to study the habits of others who have already had success in this arena. For example, if you want to be good at painting, you should study the lives and painting techniques of famous artists. If you want to play your instrument well, you need to imitate the habits of people who play your instrument at the highest level. The same applies to growing in your faith. If you want to run a great race for the Lord Jesus Christ, take time to study the lives of the people listed in Hebrews 11. Each person on the list was included because of their faith. How were they faithful to God in their lives? How did Abraham, Moses, Rahab, and many others respond in faith to their circumstances? These leaders chose a way forward that relied on and honored God.

God is interested in all the details of your life, both big and small. Life is full of decisions. Some of these decisions are bigger than others. When you purposely involve the Lord in the details of your life, you are building up your faith "muscles" to run a stronger and stronger race. You are acknowledging God's leadership and presence in your life. In what areas of your life can you lean into the Lord for wisdom, understanding, and help?

PLAYING FROM THE HEART

1. If you want to be skilled at your instrument, you need to discover musicians who are accomplished on the same instrument to imitate as role models. When you have a role model, they can give you inspiration if the going gets tough. These mentors have lots of experience in how to be successful, and they can show us clear examples of how to move forward through whatever challenges we are facing. Listen to some great artists on your instrument! Who is your favorite? What do you like about their playing? Notice how they look when they are playing their instrument. What aspects of their posture can you imitate to improve your own playing?

2. To be good at something requires consistent practice. Just like the faith heroes in Hebrews 11 chose to rely on God daily, we need to practice our instruments every day. The best way to develop a consistent practice habit is to have a plan. Start by deciding in advance when you will practice each day. You can make a practice plan for the whole week on the day after your lesson or class. If you have practice time noted on your schedule, you're much more likely to actually practice. Keep track of what things cause you to miss your practice time, and use these discoveries to improve the way in which you are scheduling your practice sessions.

3. Consistent practice paired with repetition is the perfect combination for becoming a "winner" on your instrument. You will be able to play fast, complicated music if you are willing to repeat a skill many, many times. Be joyful in practicing your tricky spots with many repetitions, knowing that you are developing finger strength, rhythmic intelligence, and excellent life habits by doing something faithfully every day.

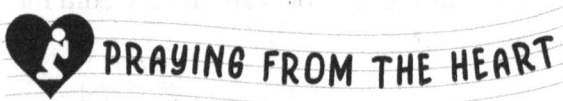

PRAYING FROM THE HEART

Dear Lord, I commit each day to You. Thank You for being with me each day and caring about even the smallest things that happen to me. Help me to run a strong race for You every day!

MY MUSIC JOURNAL

WEEK 12
BE CREATIVE!

MEMORY VERSE

So God created mankind in His own image, in the image of God He created them; male and female He created them. (Genesis 1:27)

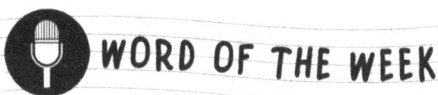

WORD OF THE WEEK

CREATIVITY: the use of the imagination or original ideas

IN TUNE WITH GOD'S WORD

Read Genesis 1:1-2:7.

SPIRITUAL THEME

If you think about the awesomeness of our world, you quickly realize how creative the God of the universe really is! For one thing, He created so many different types of plants and animals. He placed a vast numbers of stars in the universe. He's even counted every grain of sand that He made! The rotation of the earth creates a sunrise and a sunset each day and the orbit produces a cycle of seasons. This is all part of His plan and evidence of His creativity.

In Genesis 1:27, God created humankind…and the exciting part is that people were created in His own image. That means we are also creative. When you play a piece of music, you are creating a piece of musical art. After you finish playing it, your musical art is gone until the next time you create it. Every time you play a piece, your unique work of art is in existence for the duration of the piece. Your creation will never be heard again in exactly the same way, just as no two sunsets are ever the same.

Creativity is a skill we use in all areas of our life. When we solve a problem, we are using creativity. When we try new things, we are becoming more creative. As we learn to play a new piece, we are also developing our creativity when we figure out how to master a new technique using our problem-solving skills. At the same time, our creativity activates when we think about how to interpret the music and express our emotions.

We are made in God's image, and God is the Great Creator. As we develop the creative side of ourselves, we become more and more like God. Colossians 3:10 says, "… put on the new self, which is being renewed in knowledge in the image of its Creator."

 ## PLAYING FROM THE HEART

Playing from the Heart:

1. Thank God for something beautiful you noticed in nature today. Maybe it was a gorgeous skyline as the sun rose in the morning, maybe it was your adorable pet, maybe a blooming flower. Even the instrument we play was crafted by a creative person who was made in God's image, using God-created materials, like wood from a tree. God's creation is amazing, and we are blessed to have such a stunning planet.

2. Have some fun being creative with your instrument. Can you make some funny sounds that imitate birds, cats, or some other animal? Can you describe something in the room using sounds on your instrument and see if someone can guess what it is? Think of an emotion, and try to have someone guess the feeling you are trying to play. You could even compose your own piece inspired by an event, a feeling, or something you've imagined.

3. Be creative with your practice time. Can you play your piece in a room where you've never played before? What about incorporating your practice into your favorite board game in some way? For example, if you are playing checkers, each time you make a move, practice one repetition of something you are working on. If you can make a double jump or you are using a checker that has been kinged, you do it twice! Can you create your own practice chart to color or add stickers each time you practice? Can you plan your own recital, design the program, and share your music with a special audience?

 ## PRAYING FROM THE HEART

Praise the Lord for Your incredible creation! Praise the Lord for my wonderful instrument! Praise the Lord for a beautiful sunset! Praise the Lord for delicious foods! Praise the Lord for making me in His image, so I can be creative, too!

MY MUSIC JOURNAL

WEEK 13
WITH ALL YOUR HEART

📖 MEMORY VERSE

Let them praise His name with dancing and make music to Him with timbrel and harp. (Psalm 149:3)

🎤 WORDS OF THE WEEK

DANCE: a series of movements that match the speed and rhythm of a piece of music

PRAISE: the expression of approval or admiration for someone or something

🍴 IN TUNE WITH GOD'S WORD

Read Psalm 149 and 2 Samuel 6:12-15.

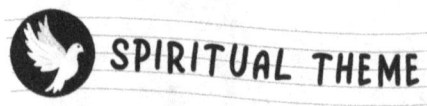
SPIRITUAL THEME

Throughout the Bible, we read about people using music to praise the Lord. Playing an instrument, dancing, and singing are all ways to express praise to God. David was celebrating with every ounce of his being when the Israelites brought the ark into the city of Jerusalem. He didn't hold back at all!

Jesus said the first and greatest commandment is, "Love the Lord your God with all your heart and with all your soul and with all your mind" (Matthew 22:37). When we praise God, we express how much we admire, honor, and worship Him. When we sing or play music, it lights up our whole brain! So, whenever we combine praise for God and music, our praise is intensified! Music brings our life experiences and emotions together in a meaningful way. We should commit to loving the Lord our God with all our heart, soul, and mind. How can we take action on this every day? Psalm 100:4 reveals a plan for getting closer to God: "Enter his gates with thanksgiving and His courts with praise." When David was bringing the ark of the covenant into Jerusalem, he was fully committed to what he was doing. In 2 Samuel 6:14-15, it says, "David was dancing before the Lord with all his might, while he and all Israel were bringing up the ark of the Lord with shouts and the sound of trumpets." Let's take a cue from David and give 100 percent of ourselves to Him each day!

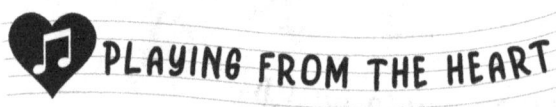
PLAYING FROM THE HEART

1. Instead of playing your review pieces this week, try dancing them! How would your movement be different between a faster-paced piece and a slower one? What is it like to experience the emotion and energy in your pieces in a new way? When you play the piece again

on your instrument, try to capture the same spirit you felt when you were dancing to it.

2. A dance locks into the rhythmic framework of the piece, mirroring the energy expressed by the composer. If it's an upbeat piece, the energy will be higher. A slower piece has the opposite effect, with a slower pulse and peaceful vibe. Being able to keep a steady beat is a critical skill for playing music well. Daily rhythm practice with a metronome or funky drumbeat will develop a strong inner pulse. You can clap, tap, say, play, or dance to a beat! Keep a practice log in your music journal to track the days you add special rhythm practice.

3. Can you do some wacky dance moves while you are playing your piece? If you can add movement to your playing, it means you are getting very good at something. We can't think about two things at once, so by adding movement we are distracting ourselves from the playing task and putting our focus on the dance moves. If you can play and dance without messing up, you are starting to get some automatic skills on your instrument. Plus, it's a whole lot of fun to bust out some moves as the Spirit moves you!

PRAYING FROM THE HEART

Lord, I want to worship You with all my heart, soul, and mind! I will play my instrument for Your glory and sing praises to You every day!

WEEK 14
A WILLING SPIRIT

 **MEMORY VERSE**

Restore to me the joy of your salvation and grant me a willing spirit, to sustain me. (Psalm 51:12)

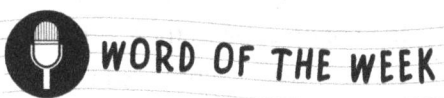 **WORD OF THE WEEK**

RESTORE: to return something to its original condition

 **IN TUNE WITH GOD'S WORD**

Read 1 Samuel 16:14-23.

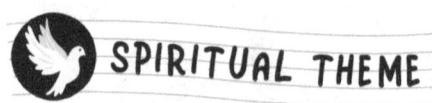 SPIRITUAL THEME

When our attitude isn't right, we should take a close look at what is making us feel this way. Sometimes the solution may be easy—you are too tired and need to get some rest. Or you are hungry and need a snack to perk yourself up. It often helps to take our problems to the Lord in prayer.

However, at other times you just don't want to do something because you're unsure about your ability to do a task. You act "grumpy" to avoid trying. If your inner "Little Grumpus" is showing its sour face, it's time to seek the Lord's help. We are all naturally rebellious, meaning we like to push against the rules. Whether your attitude problem is easy to fix or more challenging, God is always there to restore your joy and give you a willing spirit.

In 1 Samuel 16:14-23, Saul asked for someone to play the harp to soothe his bad feelings. One translation says there was "a tormenting spirit that filled him with depression and fear." Saul found great comfort in hearing David play music for him on the harp. Music can be healing, comforting, calming and uplifting. Throughout the Bible, when God's people are feeling joy, they often express their happiness with singing and music. You can use your instrument to express your emotions, happy or sad, in a deep way. Playing music can also be a way to change your mood from grumpy to cheery, or to help someone else experience its healing power.

PLAYING FROM THE HEART

1. Many people in the world today feel lonely, sad, and anxious. Use your music to bring healing and happiness to as many people as possible. Music is a form of sharing and communication. Never miss an opportunity to share your music with others. If you are willing to

use your gifts to help others, God can use you in powerful ways.

2. Your instrument can be a safe place for you to express all of your emotions. Because music engages the whole brain, your emotions will be turned on when you are playing your instrument. If you are feeling happy, play a joyful piece. If you're feeling sad, a slower, more flowing piece may match your mood better.

3. If you consistently resist daily practice, take a moment to pray about your attitude, and ask God to help you grow a willing spirit. It's important to develop the ability to be consistent with practice habits. Everyone experiences days when they are not as motivated to practice. This provides an opportunity to learn how to be consistent, even when you don't feel like it.

 **PRAYING FROM THE HEART**

Lord, give me a willing spirit. Restore my joy for all the things I have to do each day. Show me ways that I can use my music to bring healing to others.

WEEK 15
THE MESSIAH

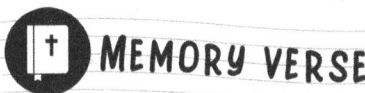 **MEMORY VERSE**

He (Jesus) told them, "This is what is written: The Messiah will suffer and rise from the dead on the third day, and repentance for the forgiveness of sins will be preached in His name to all nations, beginning at Jerusalem." (Luke 24:46-47)

 **WORD OF THE WEEK**

MESSIAH: the expected king and deliverer of the Jews

 **IN TUNE WITH GOD'S WORD**

Read Luke 24.

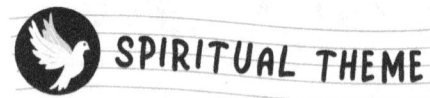# SPIRITUAL THEME

Jesus is amazing. Not only did He come to our world to teach us how to love each other and how to love God, but He was also able to heal sick people with just a word. He even raised some people from the dead—and after He was crucified, He came back to life Himself!

Right after He rose from the dead, Jesus joined two of his disciples as they were walking along a road to a village called Emmaus. He pretended not to know what they were talking about, and so they didn't realize it was Jesus. They told Him they were disappointed because they had hoped Jesus was the promised Messiah. They thought because He had died that their hopes were wrong.

But when they invited Him into their conversation, He amazed them by teaching them from the scriptures about the Messiah: the promised leader who would die for the sins of everyone, and rise from the dead. The two disciples wanted to hear more! But they still didn't recognize Jesus—until he sat down to have a meal with them. The moment they recognized him, He disappeared.

After that, they said, "Were not our hearts burning within us when he talked with us?" They felt the power and excitement that Jesus brought to their hearts. They realized He was alive again, and He really was the Messiah!

The disciples had spent lots of time with Jesus before He died, but they still didn't believe that He was the Messiah until He revealed Himself to them in a very personal way. These disciples knew God's word, so Jesus was able to use their knowledge of the Bible to help them understand what had happened to Jesus and why it had happened.

The two disciples invited Jesus to come join them for dinner. They wanted to spend more time in conversation with this man who cared about the things of God, like they did. It's wonderful to spend time at church, youth group, Bible studies, and church events to learn about Jesus. Jesus wants to be our friend and know each one of us personally. In the end, we will each need to make a decision to believe that Jesus died for our sins and rose again to give us eternal life. Have you decided to believe in Jesus Christ as your personal Savior? If you have, you are a part of God's kingdom. If you haven't, it's time to make that decision!

PLAYING FROM THE HEART

1. The two disciples had shared a common experience and were walking together along the road talking about what had happened. Learning to play an instrument is always more fun when there are friends who are doing the same thing. It is motivating to play music with friends. Try to find a group of other young musicians to join. They can help when you need extra support, and they are also there to share the fun and uplifting times.

2. The two disciples on the road to Emmaus also knew a lot about the Bible. The more you know about your instrument, the more you will enjoy it. There's so much to find out about. Do you know the history of your instrument? Did it always look the same way, or has it changed over time? Do you know any great composers who wrote music for your instrument? Have you found a favorite piece you want to play someday? Who are some famous people that play your instrument? Who is your role model and why?

3. Finally, the two disciples wanted Jesus to join them for a meal, which is a common part of everyday life. Dr. Shinichi Suzuki, a famous violin teacher, once said, "Only practice on the days you eat." In other words, make your instrument a daily part of your life, just like eating and brushing your teeth.

PRAYING FROM THE HEART

Dear Jesus, I believe You are the Messiah. Thank You for coming into my life to give me eternal life and make a home for me in Your kingdom!

MY MUSIC JOURNAL

WEEK 16
REJOICE!

MEMORY VERSE

This is the day which the Lord hath made; we will rejoice and be glad in it. (Psalm 118:24, KJV)

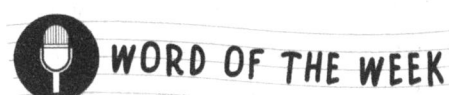

WORD OF THE WEEK

REJOICE: to feel or show that you are very happy about something

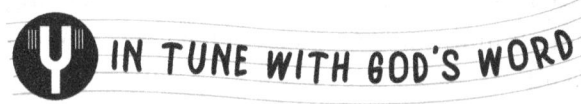

IN TUNE WITH GOD'S WORD

Read Genesis 1: 2-3.

# SPIRITUAL THEME

Did you know that there are more than 10,000 different kinds of mushrooms in the world? And that's just the ones that we know about! Scientists think there are others we haven't even discovered yet.

Guess how many different types of spiders God created? Over 45,000! That's some serious creativity! God is truly the Great Creator.

Each day we can see God's handiwork from the rising to the setting of the sun. He created the sun, moon, and stars. He created millions of different types of plants and animals, each one carefully designed by Him. And God loves it when we celebrate every single day that He has made!

God created each one of us in His image. There have never been two people who are exactly alike since the beginning of time. Even twins are slightly different. You are a beautiful and unique creation, designed by the God of the universe! Psalm 139:14 says, "I praise you because I am fearfully and wonderfully made; your works are wonderful, I know that full well." Jesus said, "And even the very hairs of your head are all numbered" (Matthew 10:30). Wow! Not only did God make billions of unique people, but He even knows the number of hairs on the heads of every person on planet earth. Now that's a God who cares about the little things.

Rejoice by praising and thanking God for the beautiful things you see in nature today. When you see a gorgeous flower, a chirping bird, or a giant oak tree, let it remind you of God's incredible care over you and the world you live in!

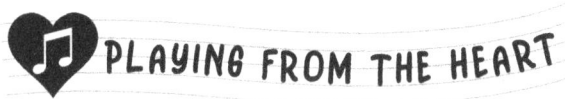 PLAYING FROM THE HEART

1. Celebrate the completion of the second quarter. Look back in this book to find the list of eight things you learned in the first quarter and add eight MORE skills you have learned in the last eight weeks. This is truly an enormous amount of learning over a short period of time. Way to go! Are there skills from the first quarter that were still difficult at the first quarter celebration, but now they feel easy? Now that you know so many pieces, which one is your favorite and why? Of the new skills you've learned this quarter, which one are you really good at? Which skill do you hope to improve in the coming eight weeks? Thank the Lord for all the support you have from your parents and teachers!

2. As you review each of the pieces you learned this quarter, can you also recite the memory verse that goes along with each piece? It's always a good idea to share your music with others by planning a "dress rehearsal" performance for friends and family. You can also share your music at a senior living center or hospital. These mini performances give you a chance to develop your on-stage skills, such as walking confidently, speaking clearly and loudly, and playing beautifully.

3. Ask your parent or caregiver to tell you a story about a time they rejoiced in what the Lord had done for them. Play their favorite piece from this quarter as a way to rejoice together in all God's love and work in our lives.

 PRAYING FROM THE HEART

Dear Jesus, I praise You because I am fearfully and wonderfully made! I praise You because your creations are wonderful. I know that full well, when I see Your beautiful creation all around me!

QUARTER TWO REVIEW

List eight new skills you learned in the last eight weeks:

1.
2.
3.
4.
5.
6.
7.
8.

WEEK 17
HAVE COURAGE!

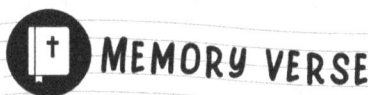 **MEMORY VERSE**

"Have I not commanded you? Be strong and courageous. Do not be afraid; do not be discouraged, for the Lord your God will be with you wherever you go." (Joshua 1:9)

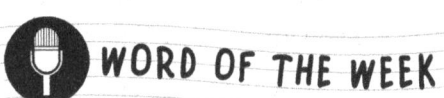 **WORD OF THE WEEK**

COURAGEOUS: to be brave in the face of danger, fear, or difficulty

 **IN TUNE WITH GOD'S WORD**

Read Joshua 1.

SPIRITUAL THEME

As Joshua prepared to lead the people of Israel into the Promised Land, God spoke some very encouraging words to him. First, God asked Joshua, "Have I not commanded you?" Then, he listed his commands:

1. Be strong. This implied that Joshua might have been feeling weak.

2. Be courageous. Joshua would need courage only if he was afraid.

3. Do not be afraid. Joshua was afraid of the unknown.

4. Don't be discouraged. The Israelites journey to take the Promised Land would take awhile, which can make enthusiasm and confidence fade over time.

God commands both Joshua and us to think about our "wilderness" experiences in a certain way. The wilderness is an untamed or less known region of the world. Your personal "wilderness" might be going to a music class, sport's practice, or a school activity for the first time. Any of those situations could be scary. Something that is unknown is generally less comfortable than something familiar. Here's the good news: No matter where you are, God is with you!

When you are afraid or discouraged, just knowing God is present with you can be very comforting. "Where can I go from Your Spirit? Where can I flee from Your presence? If I go up to the heavens, You are there; if I make my bed in the depths, You are there" (Psalm 139:7-8). As we go through life, none of us knows the future. We will have to try new things or attempt a task we aren't really sure how to do, or take a chance without knowing the outcome. However, we can count on the fact that God is with us, no matter what the future brings.

Joshua knew that God had given them the Promised Land, but the Israelites had to go into the land and claim it. "For all the promises of God in Him are Yes, and in Him Amen, to the glory of God through us" (2 Corinthians 1:20). God promises to be with us through every single moment of our lives. He has commanded us to be strong and courageous and not to be afraid and discouraged. In every new situation, we can count on God with confidence and enthusiasm!

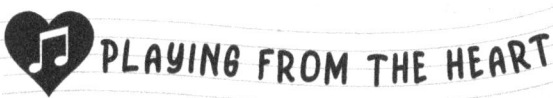
PLAYING FROM THE HEART

1. Before you start each practice session, take time to review all the things God has commanded about our attitude towards new and unknown future experiences. Say a prayer of thanks to God for being with you all the time and giving you confidence to face any new challenges. Thank Him in advance for a productive practice session.

2. Take notice of times in your lesson or class where you begin to feel nervous or worried about failing. God encourages us not to be afraid, but to approach something new with courage. The next time you have to try something in class or during practice that seems scary, immediately ask God to give you courage in that moment and jump right in!

3. Practicing every day is important to mastering an instrument. At times, the musical journey can feel discouraging. Especially when we're struggling to learn a new skill and things don't go as quickly as we'd hoped, it is normal to feel a little disappointed. But don't give up! God understands when we feel discouraged. If God is with you, you will not fail. Everything is happening at exactly the right speed. Be encouraged to continue, and be strong in your practice routine. Write a sentence in your music journal about your biggest challenge right now and also your greatest success.

♥ PRAYING FROM THE HEART

Dear Lord, thank You for giving me confidence in new situations. You are always with me, so I can rely on You when I am afraid. Help me to stay on track with my practice, so I can grow into the musician and person You made me to be.

🎵 MY MUSIC JOURNAL

WEEK 18
THE NEW IS HERE

 **MEMORY VERSE**

If you declare with your mouth, "Jesus is Lord," and believe in your heart that God raised him from the dead, you will be saved. (Romans 10:9)

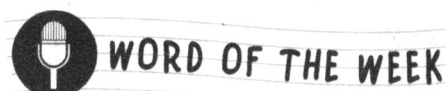 **WORD OF THE WEEK**

SAVED: delivered from sin and from spiritual death

 **IN TUNE WITH GOD'S WORD**

Read Acts 10.

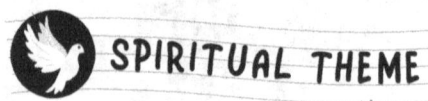 **SPIRITUAL THEME**

The story of Cornelius and his family powerfully demonstrates how God works in the lives of people who seek Him. Cornelius was a godly man. He prayed regularly and gave generously to the poor, but God wanted to have a deeper relationship with Cornelius and his family through His Son, Jesus Christ.

After God gave visions to both Cornelius and Peter, they each did what God told them to do. Peter arrived at Cornelius' home and preached the Good News about Jesus to all the relatives and close friends of Cornelius who had gathered there. He told them about how Jesus had died on the cross and then raised from the dead on the third day. Peter told them, "All the prophets testify about Him that everyone who believes in him receives forgiveness of sins through his name" (Acts 10:43). The power of the Holy Spirit helped everyone to understand what Peter was saying, so all of the people accepted the Lord Jesus Christ as their Savior.

We should imitate Cornelius by praying regularly and being generous with those less fortunate than ourselves. Cornelius was open to God and listening for His voice. Just like Cornelius and his family, God is interested in having a personal relationship with each one of us, too, but He has to get our attention first. He will bring people into our lives who tell us about Jesus and help us grow in our spiritual life. God can speak to us through a parent, a friend of the family, or someone from church. Cornelius heard God's voice through a vision and also through what Peter said to his family and friends. Because Cornelius was faithful and he sought God, he not only experienced a spiritual birth by accepting Jesus as his Savior, but he also brought his entire family and close friends to hear the Good News of Jesus Christ. Those around him also came to know Jesus Christ as their Savior.

God wants you to know about His Son Jesus who died on the cross for your sins. Because Jesus rose from the dead, when you accept Jesus as your Lord and Savior, your spirit is also raised from the dead. You become spiritually alive and receive eternal life in Jesus Christ. "Therefore, if anyone is in Christ, the new creation has come: The old has gone, the new is here!" (2 Corinthians 5:17).

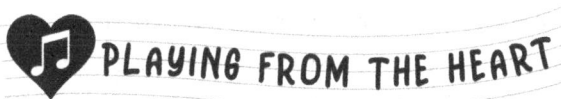 PLAYING FROM THE HEART

1. What's your newest piece to practice this week? As you make progress on your instrument, you will always have something new to work on, building on all the skills you've already learned. Each time you practice your new material this week, thank God for making you into a new creation in Christ!

2. Cornelius prayed regularly. Whenever we do something regularly, it becomes a habit. Developing a habit of practicing is a key ingredient to learning how to play an instrument well. Spend time reviewing older pieces. Ask God to renew and refresh your enthusiasm for older pieces. Have fun reviewing old pieces by playing practice games or adding something new to the practice, such as playing in a unique location or changing how you play the piece—just for fun!

3. Both Cornelius and Peter listened for what God had to say. Listening is an essential and important life skill that is developed through music. Spend time listening to the pieces you are learning and also any other music that you like. As you learn to listen more deeply, you will begin to notice more tiny details of the music. As you notice more details, your ears will help you to create the same beautiful sounds when you are playing your instrument.

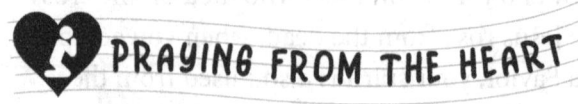 PRAYING FROM THE HEART

"Dear Jesus, I know I am a sinner. Thank You for dying on the cross for me. I accept You as my Lord and Savior. Thank You for making me part of Your family and making me a home in heaven." If this is the first time you have prayed this prayer, make sure you tell someone about your decision to accept Jesus Christ as your Lord and Savior. If you've already made this decision, tell someone about that moment and what it means to you or write about it in your music journal.

MY MUSIC JOURNAL

WEEK 19
SHOW ME YOUR WAYS

 **MEMORY VERSE**

Show me Your ways, Lord, teach me your paths. (Psalm 25:4)

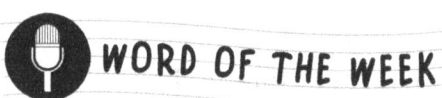 **WORD OF THE WEEK**

WISDOM: knowing how to take action using past experience, knowledge, and good judgment

 **IN TUNE WITH GOD'S WORD**

Read Acts 8:26-39.

 ## SPIRITUAL THEME

Have you ever read a book or watched a movie that amazed you—even if you didn't completely understand it? You want to keep watching or reading, but you also want to ask someone to explain it to you. That's how the Ethiopian eunuch felt as he read the Bible.

As this important financial official rode along in his chariot, he studied the words of the prophet Isaiah. During this travel time, he could have spent his time on work tasks or even just resting. But this man loved to learn. He wasn't afraid to admit it when he didn't understand, and he was willing to ask for Philip's help. Asking for help can be the easiest way to learn faster! What's even more incredible is that God knew the eunuch would need help to fully understand, so he sent Philip to him at exactly the right moment.

Knowledge is about learning something, but wisdom is about knowing how to use it. The eunuch learned about the good news of Jesus and then immediately wanted to take the next step in his walk of faith by getting baptized. He was action-oriented with his knowledge.

If you want to learn more about God, spend time reading and studying the Bible. Now, you definitely won't understand everything you read, but God will provide people to help build knowledge and answer questions. If there's something you don't understand, find someone to ask about it. Your family members who know God are a good place to start, as well as leaders in your church and Bible study groups.

 ## PLAYING FROM THE HEART

1. Be a student who seeks to learn and understand with all that you do. A good attitude towards learning will make a difference in how

quickly you learn and progress on your instrument. Before you enter your music class or lesson, determine to learn something new. If you expect to learn something, you will be actively listening for new ideas and keeping yourself open to receiving new material. After your class, tell your parent or caregiver about the most important thing you learned in the class or write it down in the music journal space for this week. This will allow you to review it later and hopefully make the learning more permanent. One of the best ways to make learning stronger is to teach it to someone else. Show someone how to do the new skill you learned, and then help them try it.

2. When you are working on a new skill, ask questions about anything you don't understand. If you are in a class, it's most likely that someone else has the same question, so by bringing it up you will be helping out your friends as well. When you ask a question, it means your brain is engaged in the learning process. Questions can also be a way to keep yourself focused. If you start to be distracted by something, ask yourself a silent question about whatever is being taught and then listen for the answer. For example, if the teacher is talking about making a good tone, ask yourself, "What makes a good tone?" Then, listen to the teacher to find out how to answer this question.

3. After you learn something new, seek ways to apply it. The eunuch wanted to know the next step for him, which turned out to be baptism. Whenever you learn something, think about how you can put it into action. If you are learning to make a better sound on your instrument and your teacher suggested a way to do this, you can immediately use this tip on all of the review pieces you play during the week. Choose specific pieces to play throughout the week that will help you focus on the new skill you have learned.

PRAYING FROM THE HEART

Lord, reveal Yourself to me in new ways today. Teach me something new about how to live my life for You. Give me opportunities to show my love for You to those around me through my actions.

MY MUSIC JOURNAL

WEEK 20
A ROARING LION

MEMORY VERSE

Be alert and of sober mind. Your enemy the devil prowls around like a roaring lion looking for someone to devour. Resist him, standing firm in the faith. (1 Peter 5:8-9a)

WORD OF THE WEEK

RESIST: to take a stand against something or someone

IN TUNE WITH GOD'S WORD

Read 1 Peter 5:5-11.

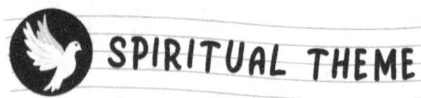 SPIRITUAL THEME

Have you ever been afraid of something and then after it was over you realized it really wasn't something to be afraid of at all? First Peter 5:8 says, "Your enemy the devil prowls around like a roaring lion looking for someone to devour." If you saw a lion walking around, it would definitely catch your attention. If that lion was ROARING, it would be that much more terrifying!

The devil is a big bully, but Jesus has authority over him. Instead of focusing on the devil's roar, resist him by standing firm in your faith in Jesus. This allows us to fight against the devil's tricks by keeping our mind focused on Jesus Christ, who has already defeated the devil. The apostle John said, "The reason the Son of God appeared was to destroy the devil's work" (1 John 3:8b).

The devil is always up to no good. In John 10:10, Jesus describes the devil as a thief that "comes only to steal and kill and destroy; I have come that they may have life, and have it to the full." The devil has three goals: stealing, killing, and destroying. But notice God's plan for us! He wants us to have life and to have it to the fullest! God's word is true, and the devil is a liar. Don't let him scare you with his bullying. You can stand against the devil with confidence since the Lord Jesus Christ has already defeated him!

 PLAYING FROM THE HEART

1. Each day, plan a mini performance into your practice session. Walk onto the pretend stage, take a bow, and get ready to play. Perform your piece, and keep going, no matter what happens. Imitate the real experience of performing as much as possible. If you can find someone to be your audience, this makes the experience even better. After you perform your piece, ask yourself: what are three specific

things you could do to improve for your performance tomorrow? This knowledge can give you wisdom to plan your practice session.

2. Have you ever been scared to try something new on your instrument? There's really no danger in trying something new. The next time you are afraid of something new, make a decision to resist your fear, have courage, and give it a try!

3. Ask your parent or caregiver about a time they were afraid. How were they courageous? Was there anything that scared them that turned out to be not quite as bad as they thought? How did God help them through the situation? Is there anything they would do differently, if it happened again? If you are afraid, take a moment to pray for strength and courage. God wants you to grow into a strong person who relies on God. Remember, our enemy the devil is already defeated!

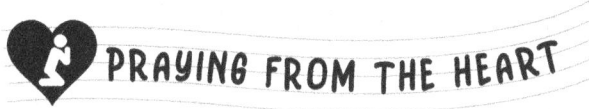# PRAYING FROM THE HEART

God, thank you for your plan to give me life and life to the fullest. Help me resist the devil and all his tricks and stand firm in my faith. I rely on You in every situation!

WEEK 21
THE ARMOR OF GOD

 **MEMORY VERSE**

Put on the full armor of God, so that you can take your stand against the devil's schemes. (Ephesians 6:11)

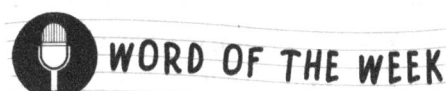 **WORD OF THE WEEK**

ARMOR: coverings worn by soldiers or warriors to protect the body in battle

 **IN TUNE WITH GOD'S WORD**

Read Ephesians 6:10-18.

# SPIRITUAL THEME

God has provided us with a full set of spiritual armor to use every day to resist the devil's schemes. It's our job to make sure we put on each piece of armor. If a soldier doesn't have each piece of the armor, they won't be fully protected.

Take time this week to study each piece of armor and why it is important. Find a piece of clothing to represent each piece of armor. As you put it on, memorize the concept that is attached. For example, the belt represents truth. Each piece of armor is listed below with a short definition and a scripture. Since there are six pieces, you can focus on one piece each day after reviewing the entire list. See if you can search the scriptures to find other places where you can learn more about truth, righteousness, readiness, faith, salvation, or the Spirit. Is there any piece of armor that you still need to put on? Which piece of armor do you want to strengthen?

Belt of truth: Knowing the difference between what is true and what is false will keep you from being deceived by the devil's lies and the ways of the world. "Then you will know the truth, and the truth will set you free" (John 8: 32).

Breastplate of righteousness: Knowing the difference between what is right and wrong will keep your heart pure to serve the Lord. "Flee the evil desires of youth and pursue righteousness, faith, love and peace, along with those who call on the Lord out of a pure heart" (2 Timothy 2:22).

Feet fitted with readiness: Be ready to serve the Lord and share the Gospel. "How beautiful on the mountains are the feet of those who bring good news, who proclaim peace, who bring good findings, who proclaim salvation, who say to Zion, 'Your God reigns!'" (Isaiah 52:7).

Shield of faith: Rely on God in all situations, and you'll be able to resist the devil's attacks. "In addition to all this, take up the shield of faith, with which you can extinguish all the flaming arrows of the evil one" (Ephesians 6:16).

Helmet of salvation: Accept Jesus Christ as your Savior, and allow His word to renew your mind. "Do not conform to the pattern of this world, but be transformed by the renewing of your mind" (Romans 12:2).

Sword of the Spirit: Know God's promises, and apply them to your daily life. "For no matter how many promises God has made, they are 'Yes' in Christ" (2 Corinthians 1:20).

PLAYING FROM THE HEART

1. Having a well-rounded practice routine is similar to putting on all the pieces of God's armor. Each part of our musical training is important and serves a purpose. Most music students practice scales, etudes or exercises, new pieces, and review pieces. As you and your parent plan your practice sessions, make sure there is time for each one of these areas. If all you practice is your new piece, you will be a weaker musician than if you spread your time out to include scales and etudes. Take time this week to organize your practice and include each area in your plan. Which area is your strongest? Which area is your weakest?

2. Being serious about learning to play your instrument means you are committed to practicing every day. Even if it's a busy day, take time to get your instrument out even for a few minutes and play something.

3. Thank God for clearly outlining the full armor of God, so you can know how to strengthen your walk with the Lord easily. Be open to allowing God to give you insights into your practice routine and help you improve those areas where you are weaker.

PRAYING FROM THE HEART

Praying from the Heart:

Dear Jesus, thank You for providing a full set of armor to protect me and make me strong. I'm putting it on every day to serve You!

MY MUSIC JOURNAL

WEEK 22
CROSSING THE RED SEA

 **MEMORY VERSE**

Moses answered the people, "Do not be afraid. Stand firm and you will see the deliverance the Lord will bring you today." (Exodus 14:13)

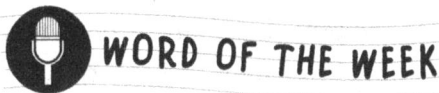 **WORD OF THE WEEK**

SALVATION: rescue from danger, difficulty or sin

 **IN TUNE WITH GOD'S WORD**

Read Exodus 14.

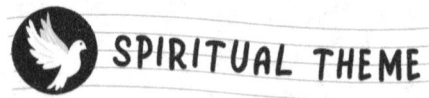

SPIRITUAL THEME

The Israelites were faced with what seemed like an impossible situation. Pharaoh had finally allowed them to leave Egypt. But as they fled, they reached the shores of the Red Sea—with no way to get across. And guess what? The Egyptians were chasing them because they had changed their mind about letting them go in the first place! The Israelites were trapped between the Red Sea and the pursuing Egyptian chariots and horsemen.

In the face of this danger, the Israelites saw God protect them in incredible ways. God led them through a pillar of cloud by day and a pillar of fire by night, which meant the Israelites could see God was with them at all times. Not only did they know God was with them, but God's pillar of cloud moved between the Israelites and the Egyptians to protect them. God told Moses that the Israelites were going to walk through the Red Sea on dry ground, and this is exactly what happened! When the Egyptians tried to do the same thing, the water walls of the Red Sea came tumbling down and covered their chariots and horsemen. They all drowned.

God was present with the Israelites and provided a way through this situation. God had told them He would bring them out of Egypt, but it didn't mean they weren't going to encounter problems and hardships along the way. The Israelites crossed the Red Sea on dry ground! This was just one of many ways God provided for them during their time in the wilderness. He always provided a way through every difficulty and challenge, so the Israelites would learn to count on Him.

If you have a goal which seems impossible or a situation that is challenging, rely on God. He is going ahead of you to help you along the way. This means you don't have to be afraid or worried, since God is with you at all times, just like He was with the Israelites. He is going before you to help you in every circumstance.

 ## PLAYING FROM THE HEART

1. Set a practicing goal, and ask God to help you achieve it. He doesn't want us to be discouraged but, rather, to be moving forward and relying on Him. Hebrews 13:8 says, "Jesus Christ is the same yesterday and today and forever." Since He doesn't change, you can have faith that He is with you to lead the way, just like He led the Israelites.

2. What's your biggest challenge right now in your musical journey? It might be a particular skill you are working to develop, such as playing a particular rhythm or playing some quick passages cleanly. It could also be related to your practice time. Do you struggle with finding a regular time each day to practice? Do you find your attitude is getting in the way of making progress on your instrument? These are all things that you can pray about and ask God to help you. God's help might come from a suggestion given in your music lesson or class for how to practice. Or, it could come through your parent or caregiver as they help you set up a practice schedule and stick to it. Or, God might change your attitude towards a challenge, which ultimately brings progress.

3. Remember how God provided a miraculous way for the Israelites to cross the Red Sea, even though it seemed impossible? Say a prayer of thanks to God for leading you through every situation. God will be there to help you meet any challenge you face in your music study and life. Celebrate God's faithfulness to His people!

 ## PRAYING FROM THE HEART

Lord, I give You thanks for leading and guiding me through every single part of my day. Even when something is hard, I know I can rely on You to bring me through it.

WEEK 23
PRACTICE PERFORMING

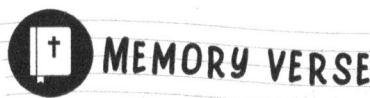
MEMORY VERSE

Teach me, Lord, the way of your decrees, that I may follow it to the end. (Psalm 119:33)

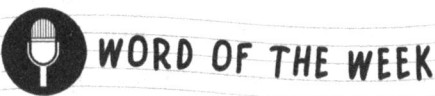
WORD OF THE WEEK

REHEARSAL: a private performance or practice session to prepare for a public appearance

IN TUNE WITH GOD'S WORD

Read Joshua 6:1-20.

SPIRITUAL THEME

God told Joshua that He would help the Israelites conquer the city of Jericho. The only problem was, Jericho was surrounded by a huge, thick wall. Joshua and his army couldn't just march right in. But God gave Joshua an unusual plan for success.

For seven days in a row, Joshua, the priests, and the army had to march around the city and blow the trumpets. In other words, they practiced or rehearsed what they would do on the seventh day when God commanded them to blow the trumpets and shout to the Lord. They made their six days of rehearsal as much like the performance as possible.

As students, we are given assignments and projects to complete. We should approach our assignments like Joshua did. God gave Joshua some very specific directions about how to bring the walls of Jericho down. Joshua gave 100 percent effort towards following these instructions, and he didn't cut corners. He could have thought, "We don't really need to carry the ark of Lord around this whole city six times. It would be easier to just walk around without it. We'd still be walking around the city, so we're still doing most of the assignment." Not a chance! He followed the directions God gave him exactly and the result was phenomenal!

Throughout our life, our goal is to know Jesus Christ more deeply and become more like Him. By studying God's word, we can learn how to grow spiritually and follow Jesus. God can speak to us through His word about things we need to improve in our lives and how we can better reflect His character in our daily lives. In order for God to speak to you through His word, you have to be spending time reading it and getting to know what the Bible says. Just like Joshua, we need to know the plan and then follow it!

PLAYING FROM THE HEART

1. When we rehearse something daily, it becomes easier. Practice also prepares us for the big performance day. There are several ways to prepare for a performance. Imagine if you played a concert every day during the week before your actual performance! These "preparation" concerts during the week before your actual performance could take place at your home for family members, at a retirement home for elderly residents, or in your room for a crowd of stuffed animals or dolls. Whatever the performance location, create an environment as similar to the concert atmosphere as possible and try to play the pieces in exactly the order you will perform them at the performance. You will be so ready for your actual performance if you practice "performing"!

2. As you think about your playing, are there any directions your teacher gave you about how to play your instrument that you are ignoring? It might seem like a small thing to hold your arms in a certain way, but in actuality, how you use your arms is one of the most important aspects of playing well. Spend some practice time listing out the tiny details you've learned about how to hold your instrument well. Are there any directions that you aren't following? Can you create a practice plan to fix these details of your performance that you have been overlooking?

3. Reviewing your older pieces is also a great way to remind yourself of past skills you have learned and even strengthen this technique even more. Sometimes a review piece can feel a lot easier than when it was being learned the first time. You can do the same thing with several memory verses from earlier weeks in this devotional. Reviewing God's promises to you strengthens your faith and understanding of Him. Select a memory verse to say out loud before playing a review piece.

♥ PRAYING FROM THE HEART

Dearest Lord Jesus, teach me Your ways. I want to bring my actions into line with Your ways and follow Your example.

 MY MUSIC JOURNAL

WEEK 24
SHOW YOUR APPRECIATION

 **MEMORY VERSE**

You will go out in joy and be led forth in peace; the mountains and hills will burst into song before you, and all the trees of the field will clap their hands. (Isaiah 55:12)

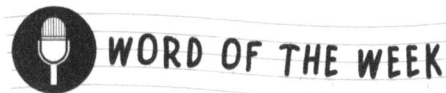 **WORD OF THE WEEK**

APPRECIATION: a feeling or expression of admiration, approval, or gratitude

 **IN TUNE WITH GOD'S WORD**

Read Isaiah 55.

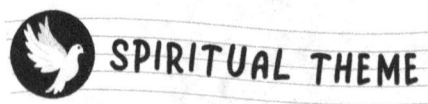

SPIRITUAL THEME

God gives us a wonderful promise in this week's memory verse: joy and peace! Isaiah 55:11 says, "So is my word that goes out from my mouth: It will not return to me empty, but will accomplish what I desire and achieve the purpose for which I sent it." We can go about our day with joy because God is leading us forward in peace. Isaiah compares God's word to rain and snow. Rain and snow water the earth and make it produce plants. God's promises are exactly the same. They will produce a result. He is faithful and true to fulfill His promises.

As you read through this chapter in Isaiah, look for the actions God invites us to take: Come, listen, see, seek, and call. If we decide to "come" to God, our next task will be to pay attention. By listening and watching, we will see God working in our lives. Because we know God is active in our lives, we will want to continue to seek Him and call upon Him in every circumstance. It is such a blessing to have a God who cares about each one of us personally!

PLAYING FROM THE HEART

1. Celebrate the completion of the third quarter. Find the list of 16 things you learned in the first and second quarters. Now, add eight MORE skills you have learned in the last eight weeks. Wow! You should celebrate the huge amount of learning you have done over the last 24 weeks. Think about some of the skills from the first quarter that you can now do very easily! Look at the skills from the second quarter. Are there any of these skills that you were struggling with during the last quarter, but you now have improved through your practicing? Review the eight new skills you have added to the list. Put a star next to the ones you can do the best. Circle the ones that

still need more practice. Use the circled items to plan your practice goals over the final eight weeks of class.

2. The memory verse says that the trees of the field will clap their hands. Clapping is a way of showing praise and enjoyment. That's why the audience at your performance is clapping! They have enjoyed your performance and also want to give you praise for all you've accomplished through your hard work. Who do you know who deserves applause? Are there any people who make a big difference in your life? Find a way to show your appreciation for this person, and tell them thank you for the good things they bring to your life.

3. Reflect on the blessings you have received from God during this last quarter. What are you thankful for? What are some ways you think you have learned about Jesus in the past weeks that have been meaningful to you? Make sure you tell the Lord how grateful you are for His blessings in your life!

PRAYING FROM THE HEART

Thank You, God, for all Your blessings on me and my family. I'm so grateful for my teachers, parents, and family members who support me on my musical journey. Please bless them in a big way!

QUARTER THREE REVIEW

List eight new skills you learned in the last eight weeks:

1.
2.
3.
4.
5.
6.
7.
8.

WEEK 25
SUPERHERO SKILLS

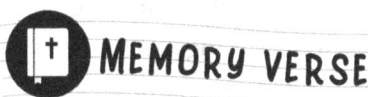 **MEMORY VERSE**

For He is the living God and He endures forever; His kingdom will not be destroyed, His dominion will never end. He rescues and He saves; He performs signs and wonders in the heavens and on the earth. (Daniel 6:26b-27a)

 **WORD OF THE WEEK**

RESCUE: to free from confinement, danger, or evil

 **IN TUNE WITH GOD'S WORD**

Read Daniel 6.

 SPIRITUAL THEME

Daniel made a decision early in his life that he was going to live for God. No matter what the circumstances, he stood firm in his beliefs, even if it meant he might get in trouble. And God was there to rescue him in every situation! In this story, Daniel would not follow the king's rule against praying. A group of leaders caught Daniel praying to God for help and turned him in to the king. Even though the king didn't really want to do it, he had to follow through with the law he had put into place. Daniel was thrown into the lion's den.

Miraculously, God shut the mouths of the lions, and Daniel was alive and well in the morning when they opened the lion's den. Imagine spending the night with a bunch of lions and coming out alive! Because Daniel lived a life dedicated to knowing and serving God, God protected him. In Daniel 10:12, God said to Daniel in a vision, "Do not be afraid, Daniel. Since the first day that you set your mind to gain understanding and to humble yourself before your God, your words were heard, and I have come in response to them."

Just as God protected Daniel, He will protect you! God answered his prayers for help, because Daniel had "set his mind" to understanding and "humbled himself." Daniel is an excellent example of a real life superhero. He lived his life in service to God. The Bible says people noticed that he was completely trustworthy and never corrupt or negligent (Daniel 6:4). This meant he was dependable and honest, made good and moral decisions, and always took care of all his responsibilities. You could count on Daniel to do the right thing.

Trying to imitate the great characteristics of a superhero of the faith like Daniel is a great way to start in your walk with the Lord. Ask yourself:

1. Are you always dependable? In other words, do you do what you say you will do?

2. Are you honest? Do you tell the truth even if you think you might get in trouble?

3. Are you responsible? Do you take care of all the things you are supposed to do?

PLAYING FROM THE HEART

1. The same character traits that make you like Daniel will help you when studying an instrument. Being responsible to practice daily and showing up consistently to music lessons and classes builds habits that are beneficial in all areas of life. Can you be as consistent as possible in your practice plan in order to achieve your goals? Dedicate yourself to developing your own superhero skills!

2. When we humble ourselves before God, it means we realize we can't do it on our own. We need His help. Daniel asked for God's help when he needed it, and he was rescued from the lion's den. Remember to ask for help when you need it. Of course, you can always pray to God for help, but your parents, teachers, and caregivers are there to help, too. Asking for help when you need it is one of the smartest skills you can develop for success in life.

3. Daniel made a decision and then stuck to it. Make a decision that you will learn to play your instrument well. Once you've made this positive decision, you will be less likely to allow yourself to make excuses for not practicing. Also, it's easier to get discouraged and give up when you haven't truly committed to something. When you make a decision and stick to it, you'll become a superhero like Daniel. Write your commitment in your music journal.

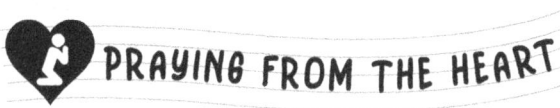

PRAYING FROM THE HEART

Lord, I know I need Your help every single day. I have made a commitment to serve You throughout my life.

WEEK 26
ALL THINGS WORK TOGETHER

 **MEMORY VERSE**

And we know that in all things God works for the good of those who love him, who have been called according to his purpose. (Romans 8:28)

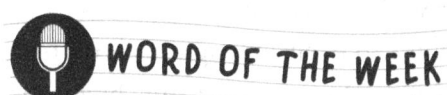 **WORD OF THE WEEK**

PURPOSE: the reason for which something is done or created

 **IN TUNE WITH GOD'S WORD**

Read Genesis 45.

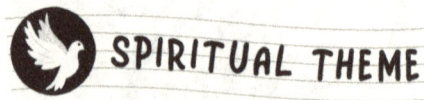 SPIRITUAL THEME

Spiritual Theme:

Joseph had become a strong leader in Egypt during a famine, a time when there was not enough food. He relied on God to help him solve problems, and He followed God's directions. During the years when there was plenty of food, Joseph set up a system of food storage, which later allowed him to save many people by giving them food when they needed it.

Joseph's path to leadership was not an easy one, though! His jealous brothers sold him into slavery in Egypt. He was thrown into prison after his master's wife lied about him. In prison, he helped all of the inmates, but when they had an opportunity to help him to get out of prison, they forgot about him. But God had a purpose for Joseph's life and revealed to Joseph the meaning of a dream the king had. The king was so thankful that he put Joseph in charge of preparing Egypt to face the coming challenge his dream had revealed.

Because Joseph obeyed God's direction in every situation, he ended up saving the people of Egypt, as well as his entire family. When his family came to Egypt to get food, it had been so long since they had seen Joseph they didn't recognize him. As Joseph tearfully hugged his brothers with forgiveness and love, he said, "You intended to harm me, but God intended it for good to accomplish what is now being done, the saving of many lives" (Genesis 50:20). Joseph fulfilled God's purpose for his life through his obedience and service to God no matter the circumstance.

Romans 8:28 promises that "... in all things God works for the good of those who love him, who have been called according to his purpose." When Jesus died and rose again, He sent the Holy Spirit to teach us and remind us of His promises. Even though you can't see the Holy Spirit, He is working undercover in every situation to bring all things together in a good way for those people who have accepted

Jesus Christ as their Savior!

Just like Joseph, you will find yourself in many different types of situations throughout your life. Whether the situation is comfortable or uncomfortable, you can choose to continue learning and growing in your relationship with Christ. Every music lesson or class can teach us something about ourselves beyond the musical skills we are supposed to learn. When a performance or class session doesn't go exactly the way you want it to go, you can still learn something from it. The Holy Spirit will use every situation to build up your character and make you more like Jesus.

PLAYING FROM THE HEART

1. After every class or lesson, give yourself a score of 1 to 10. A score of 10 means you were totally engaged in the class and working hard to improve your skills. If your score is closer to 1, you can ask the Holy Spirit to help you to focus and learn in every situation. Can you achieve a higher score today than you did yesterday? What's your total for the week? Keep track over the quarter to see if you can improve or maintain a high level of effort and good attitude. God can use every class and lesson to grow your abilities!

2. Ask your parent or caregiver to tell you about a time when something bad turned out to be good, thanks to God's help. Were there any special promises that the Holy Spirit brought to their mind to help them through the situation?

3. Ask your parent or caregiver to tell a story about a time when they learned an important lesson about themselves through an experience which wasn't ideal. What did the Holy Spirit teach them? Can you think of a time when a practice or a performance didn't go the way you had hoped? What did the Holy Spirit teach you through this experience?

♥ PRAYING FROM THE HEART

Dear Lord, thank You for bringing good out of every situation in my life. Remind me of Your promise to comfort and teach me through all my experiences to make me more like You.

🎵 MY MUSIC JOURNAL

WEEK 27
CITIZEN OF HEAVEN

 **MEMORY VERSE**

Your kingdom is an everlasting kingdom, and your dominion endures through all generations. (Psalm 145:13a)

 **WORD OF THE WEEK**

KINGDOM: a community led by a king or queen

 **IN TUNE WITH GOD'S WORD**

Read Psalm 145.

SPIRITUAL THEME

In earlier times, each country was ruled by a king or queen, and the people who lived in their kingdom knew they were in charge.

Jesus is the ruler of our spiritual kingdom. He loves each one of us very much and wants to make sure we become part of His kingdom. In fact, He was willing to give His life for us, so we could have eternal life and become a citizen of heaven.

Our sins have separated us from God and placed us outside of the kingdom of God. Jesus opened the door to His kingdom by His death on the cross. When Jesus died on the cross and rose again three days later, God completed His plan to forgive our sins. Jesus is now on His throne in heaven and welcomes anyone who puts their faith and trust in Him into His kingdom. After we accept Christ, we become citizens in His kingdom and are freed from our sins!

In order to become a citizen in Jesus' kingdom, you have to accept Him as your Lord and Savior. Do you believe Jesus died for your sins and rose again on the third day? Do you accept Him as your Lord? Since He is the King and you are a citizen in His kingdom, are you willing to live by His laws and allow Him to lead you through life?

PLAYING FROM THE HEART

1. In your music class, there is a leader. Are you listening to the leader and following their directions? As a good citizen of class, you should follow the rules and listen carefully to what you are supposed to do. How can you be an even better citizen of your music class?

2. At home, your parent or caregiver is the leader. How can you become a better helper at home? Make a list of three things you could do to make a difference in your home. Maybe it's finishing all your chores on time or getting ready for bed without complaining or

giving maximum effort during each practice session. Whatever it is, find a way to be the best member of your family that you can be.

3. The descending notes of a scale can remind you that Jesus came down from heaven to die on the cross for our sins. So celebrate what the King has done for you! Each time you practice your scales, say a prayer of thanks to God for making you a citizen of His kingdom.

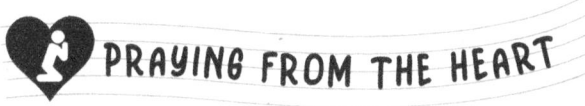

PRAYING FROM THE HEART

Dear Jesus, thank You so much for making a way for me to be a part of Your kingdom! You are my Lord and Savior!

WEEK 28
RELYING ON GOD

MEMORY VERSE

Show me your ways, Lord, teach me your paths. (Psalm 25:4)

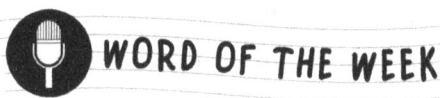
WORD OF THE WEEK

RELY: to depend upon and to have confidence based on experience

IN TUNE WITH GOD'S WORD

Read 1 Samuel 10 (Saul's anointing) and 1 Samuel 16:1-13 (David's anointing).

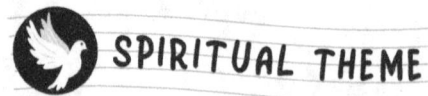
SPIRITUAL THEME

God chose both David and Saul to be kings of Israel, but their paths were very different. David had many experiences that prepared him to be the king of Israel. When he was young, he was responsible for caring for his father's flock of sheep. He had to overcome some very scary challenges to protect the sheep. He fought a bear and a lion!

Defeating these dangerous animals prepared him to fight Goliath later in his life. Each challenge was a little bit bigger and a little bit tougher. But God had a plan for David's life—to be king someday. As he went through these challenges, David learned how to be a wise leader and to continue to rely on God to guide him throughout his life.

Saul was also chosen by God to be king. Things went alright for a while, but then Saul decided to start making his own decisions, instead of listening to what God had to say. God planned for both of these men to be king of Israel, but the result of each of their reigns was very different. David was a man after God's own heart. Saul, on the other hand, decided to do things his own way.

In the same way, God has a plan for your life and will prepare you to meet whatever challenges you face. Each experience we have can help us grow into a person that is more like Jesus. We can also go the opposite direction and ignore God's lessons. Sometimes we know what is right, but we still do what is wrong. At other times, we begin to believe we create our success by our own efforts rather than with God's help. Staying the course with God means relying on Him in every situation, so we can learn His ways and fulfill His plan for our life to the fullest!

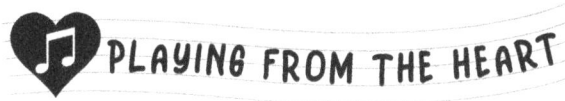 PLAYING FROM THE HEART

1. You are playing an instrument, which requires hard work, practice and commitment. You can be confident that God has given you the tools you need to meet any challenge, including those skills you are developing on your instrument. Don't give up or get discouraged when you encounter something difficult! When we tackle something hard, we grow our patience, confidence, and willingness to stick with something.

2. Your teachers were once students, too. They had to go through the same challenges you are facing when they were learning to play. You can rely on them to know the best ways to learn something new on your instrument. They can show you the way and encourage you through the rough spots that every young musician encounters. Be sure to listen to their instructions and follow them.

3. Dedicate each practice session to the Lord. Pray before you practice, and thank Him for His help after each session is finished.

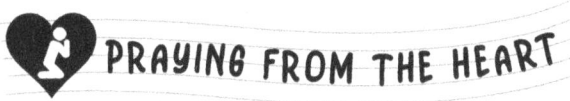 PRAYING FROM THE HEART

Dear Lord, Your word says that You go before me and come after me. Thank You for leading me through an effective practice session and surrounding me with Your love.

WEEK 29
FOLLOWING DIRECTIONS

MEMORY VERSE

"Now I know that there is no God in all the world except in Israel." (2 Kings 5:15b)

WORD OF THE WEEK

PRIDEFUL: a feeling that you are more important or better than other people

IN TUNE WITH GOD'S WORD

Read 2 Kings 5:1-15.

# SPIRITUAL THEME

God provided Naaman with a solution for healing his leprosy. God's plan for healing Naaman included a servant girl from Israel who was a victim of war. She was serving Naaman's wife and mentioned a prophet from Samaria she thought could help. Naaman decided to explore this suggestion, but instead of searching for the prophet, he decided to approach his own boss, who proceeded to give him a letter for the King of Israel. Naaman had his own ideas about who to approach. Rather than trying to find the prophet the servant girl recommended, he decided to go to the most important people he knew in both his region and Israel.

Naaman scared the King of Israel with his request for healing because the King didn't have any idea how to help. When Elisha heard about it and told the king to send Naaman his way, Naaman still had his own ideas about how he wanted the solution to come. In fact, it made him angry that Elisha sent a messenger instead of coming out to greet him. Naaman thought of himself as such an important figure that he determined Elisha should have respected him enough to deliver the message himself.

He was so prideful and self-important that he didn't even want to follow Elisha's simple directions delivered by the messenger. In order to cleanse his leprosy, he had to dip seven times in the river Jordan. Once again, Naaman started complaining. He didn't like the river he was supposed to use, and he didn't like doing something repetitively to achieve the result. Basically, he wanted a different solution all around. Thankfully, his friends were able to convince him to try dipping seven times in the Jordan River.

As a result, he was healed. More importantly, he came to know the Lord. Naaman declared, "Now I know that there is no God in all the world except in Israel" (I Kings 5:15).

How can we learn from Naaman's story? Do you ever argue with your teachers, parents, or caregivers when they ask you to do something? Do you ever resist directions you are given which you know would help you improve? We need to practice having a good attitude and giving full effort in everything we do in our daily lives. If you enjoy being a leader like Naaman, you also need to be a good listener and willing to take direction from others when necessary. The best leaders are willing to hear suggestions from all the people around them, no matter what their role, and then wisely use help from wherever it comes.

♪ PLAYING FROM THE HEART

1. When someone asks you to do something this week, pay attention to your reaction. Try to notice your own attitude. Do you ever argue or resist doing something your teacher, parent, or caregiver asks you to do? Or do you cheerfully do what they ask? Do you roll your eyes and grumpily do the task? Or do you look for ways to cheerfully help your parents and teachers? This week, notice how you respond to directions from adults. See if you can decide to have a positive attitude. The more willing you are to follow directions, the quicker you will learn!

2. It can be hard to practice something over and over. Repetition, even though it may seem tiring, is the best way to get really good at something. Are you like Naaman who didn't want to dip seven times even though he knew it could have a very positive effect? Find three tricky segments in your practice that you can practice repetitively this week. Set a number of times to practice each segment, and set a goal to complete these every day. Keep track of your repetitions in your music journal. Not only will you be practicing the challenging skills you need to improve, but you will also be practicing how to be disciplined, a key ingredient of success in life!

3. Practice listening carefully to all the directions you are given and then trying to follow them exactly. If you need to change something about the way you are playing your instrument, keep focused on that

change no matter how slowly you need to go. By carefully listening and following directions, you will become a better musician!

PRAYING FROM THE HEART

Dear Jesus, I want to be a good listener and be willing to follow Your directions. Help me to continue to grow an attitude of respect for my teachers and parents.

MY MUSIC JOURNAL

WEEK 30
FISHERS OF MEN

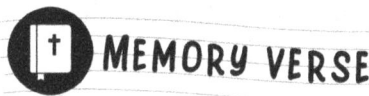

MEMORY VERSE

But as for me and my household, we will serve the Lord. (Joshua 24:15b)

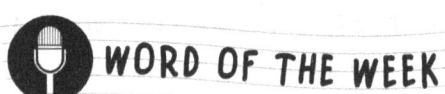

WORD OF THE WEEK

SERVE: to be useful and helpful

IN TUNE WITH GOD'S WORD

Read Luke 5:1-11.

 SPIRITUAL THEME

When the disciples first met Jesus, they were working as fishermen. Jesus called them away from their daily jobs as fishermen and asked them to join Him. However, he also helped them catch a lot of fish. Every day we have the opportunity to serve the Lord in all our activities.

The Lord is working all the time and in all situations. If we are open to the Holy Spirit's direction, we can serve Him throughout our day, even while we are doing our regular tasks.

Maybe there is someone in your class who is feeling left out and doesn't seem to have any friends. You can reach out to introduce yourself and try to make a new friend.

Maybe your parent, caregiver, brother, or sister has a really hard chore to do, and you could help them to finish it. The more people who help, the easier the work.

Maybe you have noticed a classmate who is feeling discouraged. You can let them know that you feel discouraged sometimes, too. When there is someone to go through a difficulty with you, it can take away the discouragement of walking the path alone.

These are all examples of everyday life situations, just like the fishermen in the story had worked all night without catching anything. However, when Jesus came along, He helped them catch a lot of fish, but He also told them they would be "fishers of men." This means they would be helping people that they encountered in their daily lives to know Jesus and have a relationship with God. We are supposed to show Jesus to the world by how we act and what we do. Being a friend, helping with chores, and encouraging others are all Christlike activities. How can you be more like Jesus in your daily life and serve Him in every situation?

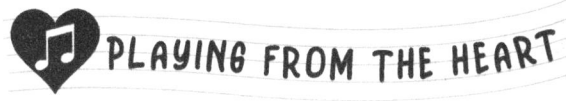 PLAYING FROM THE HEART

1. Pray for the Holy Spirit to make you aware of people you can help in your daily life. Each situation you're in—whether it's a music class, school recess, or evening activity with your family—God is there, and He's working. Stay open to His direction, so you can join Him in His work.

2. Know that God will help you to accomplish all the things you need to do each day. Just like He helped the disciples catch more fish than they'd ever caught before, He's interested in helping you with all the daily activities you are involved in.

3. Thank the Lord in advance for showing you how to be an example of Jesus Christ to those around you and for making you aware of people who need to feel God's love through your helpfulness, encouragement, or friendliness.

 PRAYING FROM THE HEART

Lord, Make me aware of those people in my life I can help. Keep me focused not only on accomplishing my goals, but also showing Christ to those around me through my actions.

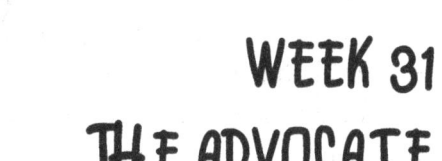

WEEK 31
THE ADVOCATE

MEMORY VERSE

Jesus said: "But the Advocate, the Holy Spirit, whom the Father will send in my name, will teach you all things and will remind you of everything I have said to you." (John 14:26)

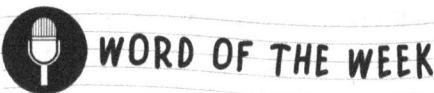
WORD OF THE WEEK

ADVOCATE: someone who promotes, supports, and defends a cause or another person

IN TUNE WITH GOD'S WORD

Read 1 Samuel 3.

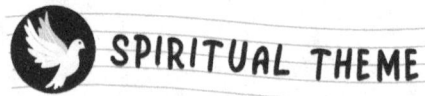 SPIRITUAL THEME

Samuel was a young boy when God called him. His mother had placed him in training under the priest Eli. Samuel was listening for God and learning about the things of the Lord. His life in the temple was focused on God. When he first heard God's voice, Samuel didn't know who it was! A more experienced follower of the Lord, his teacher Eli, had to help Samuel understand the Lord's call on his life. After Samuel learned to recognize God's voice, he continued to grow with God. "The Lord continued to appear at Shiloh, and there He revealed Himself to Samuel through His word" (1 Samuel 3:21).

We can learn to recognize God's voice by studying the Bible. As a student of God's word, God will reveal Himself to us through His word, just like He did with Samuel. The Bible will become your best resource for becoming more like Him. Since the Bible is a very big book and has lots of stories and guidance for becoming more like Jesus, we have a lot to learn. No worries! This is where the Advocate or Holy Spirit comes in to support, promote and defend us. We can rely on the Holy Spirit to catch our attention and open our eyes to the truth while we are reading the Bible. The Holy Spirit will help us see clearly the things we might need to change in our lives in order to be more like Jesus.

God wants to speak to us directly through His Word. To hear His voice, we need to set aside time every day to read His Word and listen for the Holy Spirit. Just like the memory verse says, the Holy Spirit will teach us and remind us of God's promises and His faithfulness to those promises.

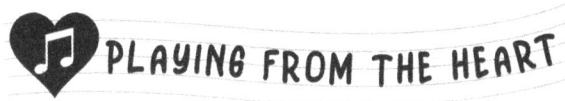 PLAYING FROM THE HEART

1. As you prepare for the final performance of the fourth quarter, review all the directions your teacher has given you about how to play each piece, the correct posture, and even instructions about how to act when you are taking the stage to perform your pieces. Are there any details of the directions that you need to follow more carefully? Did you miss anything? What pieces on the program need special attention throughout the week to be able to play them at the highest level possible?

2. Play a special performance of your pieces sometime during the week. Set one goal to work on throughout the performance. Count how many pieces in which you reached your goal. Example goals might be: 1) Playing the whole piece with all the dynamics; 2) Performing with excellent posture; or 3) Including all the correct articulations (short, long, accents, etc.). Were you able to focus on your goal and make it happen throughout the performance?

3. For each piece on the program, try to remember one or two important things your teacher has said about how to play that piece well. Make this list of things to remember early in the week so you can get really good at following all of your teacher's suggestions before the big performance!

 PRAYING FROM THE HEART

Dear Lord, Thank You for revealing Yourself to me through study of Your Word. I want to know You better each day.

WEEK 32
A GOOD WORK

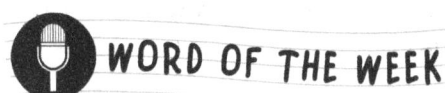 **MEMORY VERSE**

Being confident of this, that he who began a good work in you will carry it on to completion until the day of Christ Jesus. (Philippians 1:6)

WORD OF THE WEEK

COMPLETE: having all necessary parts, elements, or steps

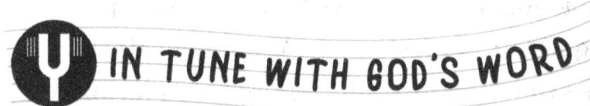 **IN TUNE WITH GOD'S WORD**

Read Philippians 1:3-11.

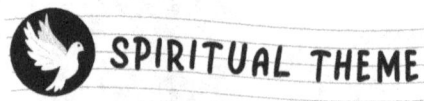 SPIRITUAL THEME

The memory verse promises that God will complete His plan for your life. All things are working together in your life for your good (see Romans 8:28). God has a plan to prosper you, to give you hope and a bright future (see Jeremiah 29:11). Even when things sometimes seem tough, God uses every experience to make you into a better person. God wants us to grow in our love for others, our knowledge of Him, and wisdom in how we apply His word to our lives.

As we bring this 32-week study to an end, think about how much you have grown in both your musical skills and your knowledge of the Lord Jesus Christ.

Even though you have gained much knowledge and skill, you still have so much more to learn. The memory verse says, "He who has BEGUN a good work…." It's exciting to know there's more to come. Keep learning as you continue your musical and spiritual journey.

"The Lord bless you and keep you; the Lord make His face shine on you, and be gracious to you; the Lord turn His face towards you and give you peace" (Numbers 6:24-26).

 PLAYING FROM THE HEART

1. Celebrate the completion of the In Tune with God's Word devotional and four quarters of music study. You should already have a list of 24 things you've learned since you started playing your instrument. Now, it's time to add your final eight items to complete your list of successes. Remember how much you needed to learn to play to get to this point in your musical journey and celebrate your growing ability! This is a huge accomplishment!

2. After you've celebrated your accomplishments, think about what's next. What do you think are your strengths? Maybe you are especially good at rhythm or note reading or making a beautiful tone. What are the skills you want to improve? Make a list of two or three things you would like to improve or learn. Is there a piece you know that you'd like to play on your instrument? Thinking about the future and what you'd like to learn is a great way to motivate yourself to keep practicing and set new goals.

3. Celebrate what God has done in your life through this study! Are there several stories you can share about ways God has helped you over the last 32 weeks? Who has been a special blessing to you? How can you show them your appreciation? Pray for each one of your classmates and teachers, and ask God to give them many more blessings.

PRAYING FROM THE HEART

Thank You, Jesus, for bringing me through to this final performance. I am so grateful for all the lessons I've learned from Your word. Bless my friends, teachers, and family with joy and peace as we continue our musical journey!

Quarter Four Review

List eight new skills you learned in the last eight weeks:

1.
2.
3.
4.
5.
6.
7.
8.

ABOUT THE AUTHOR

Ruth Meints has been the Executive Director of the Omaha Conservatory of Music since 2005 and authored the String Sprouts curriculum launched in 2013. String Sprouts enrolls over one thousand preschoolers from underserved areas and provides an instrument for all five years of instruction at no cost to the families.

She currently teaches violin and viola at the Omaha Conservatory and conducts various workshops around the country in violin/viola pedagogy and music education, integrating current neuroscience findings into music teaching. While at the Omaha Conservatory, she has developed many music education programs, such as OCM's Summer Institutes, Winter Festival Orchestra, a full music program at the St. Augustine Indian Mission School, as well as the Inside the Mind of the Artist recital and master class series.

Her teaching experience has included head of the string department at Azusa Pacific University and faculty at Biola University in the Los Angeles area, as well as faculty at San Jose Talent Education, Omaha Talent Education, and Artist-Faculty at the Omaha Conservatory of Music. In 2016, Ruth was given the Governor's Arts Award for excellence in arts education sponsored by Nebraska Arts Council and Nebraska Cultural Endowment. In 2019, she also presented a TedXOmaha talk entitled "Music, Preschoolers, and Poverty."

Ruth received her Bachelor of Music in Violin Performance from the University of Nebraska-Lincoln and her Master of Music degree with an emphasis in Suzuki pedagogy from Southern Illinois University-Edwardsville with John Kendall, pioneer in bringing the Suzuki philosophy to the United States.

ABOUT STRING SPROUTS

In 2013, the Omaha Conservatory of Music launched an innovative new program called String Sprouts aimed at creating equitable access to the arts for young children growing up in under-resourced areas.

The curriculum, authored by Ruth Meints, is based on foundational tenets from both the Suzuki and the El Sistema philosophies. Children enroll in the program at age three to four, and caregiver involvement is mandatory.

Instruments are provided for each student at no cost to the families for all five years of the program. The group class lessons are held exclusively in underserved areas. This community-wide initiative gives children the opportunity to learn a stringed instrument with a ready-to-use curriculum and engaging new repertoire by composer Dryden Meints. (String Odyssey is available at www.meintsproductions.com.)

In 2019, the Omaha Conservatory's String Sprouts program enrolled over 1,300 children and continues to grow. Program evaluation has shown positive results in improving school-readiness skills and developing stronger family relationships. The program equips children with valuable life skills such as discipline, confidence, and persistence, as well as fostering a lifelong love of music. Dr. Shinichi Suzuki, music educator and philosopher, stated, "I think that all of the people who love art, those who teach art, and all of you, should burn with the obligation to save the world. It is necessary to be concerned about the importance of educating a really beautiful spirit." String Sprouts is an extraordinary journey that moves the world one step closer to making this dream a reality.

If you would like more information about how to start your own String Sprouts program or register for String Sprouts teacher training courses, please contact the Omaha Conservatory at www.stringsprouts.org.

www.ingramcontent.com/pod-product-compliance
Lightning Source LLC
Chambersburg PA
CBHW011319080526
44589CB00018B/2730